AMERICA,
DO WE REALLY LOVE HER?

WILLIAM T. SMITH

Copyright © 2023 by William T. Smith. All rights reserved.

All rights reserved. No part of this book may be reproduced or transmitted in any form or by any means, electronic or mechanical, including photocopying, recording, or by any information storage and retrieval system without express written permission from the author, except in the case of brief quotations embodied in critical reviews and certain other noncommercial uses permitted by copyright law.

Published in the United States of America

Brilliant Books Literary
137 Forest Park Lane Thomasville
North Carolina 27360 USA

ISBN:
Paperback: 979-8-88945-284-3
Ebook: 979-8-88945-285-0

DEDICATION

To my brother Jim; who served in the Army.

MY THANKS

A special thanks to the soldiers who keeps us free.
A special thanks to the ministers who preach God's Word.
A special thanks to all volunteers, your service is appreciated.
A very special thanks to the Holy Spirit, for inspiring me.

A NOTE FROM THE AUTHOR

I wish to thank my Lord and Savior (Jesus of Nazareth) for this book. My hope is that our elected officers in all branches of the government will listen to that still voice of Jesus. If they do not know who Jesus is personally; I pray that the Holy Spirit will prick there hearts to come to him. In ether case I pray that the Holy Spirit will guide them in the right way to keep America free.

The Poems, Psalms, Proverbs, or Parables are my thoughts in this book.
Bible verses came from the King James Version.
Things I read in other books and newspapers.
Things I heard on TV, news, and radio.
Quotes are followed by the persons name.
Young Students Learning Library
Illustrated World Encyclopedia

PLEDGE TO THE AMERICAN FLAG

I pledge allegiance to the flag of the United States of America, and to the Republic for which it stands. One nation under God, indivisible, with liberty and justice for all.

PLEDGE TO THE CHRISTIAN FLAG

I pledge allegiance to the Christian Flag and to the Savior for whose Kingdom it stands. One Savior, crucified, risen, and coming again with life and liberty to all who believe.

PLEDGE TO THE BIBLE

I pledge allegiance to the Bible, God's Holy Word, I will make it a lamp unto my feet and a light unto my path and will hide its words in my heart that I might not sin against God.

HEAR YE, HEAR YE

Hear Ye, Hear Ye: A cry to Ole United States of America.
You have forgotten what the constitution has to say.
Our dogs knows where to go and who their masters are.
Our nation has forgotten who has brought them this far.
Our cats will crawl up and lay beside their master.
You politicians get elected and forget about the voters.
Oh, United States of America, remember our heritage.
When we were out gunned, and out numbered by the English.
Our faith in God brought us to victory, and the victory march.
Every battle, every victory was won by our Lord Jesus, not us.
We used to own our plants, factories, oil production and business.
Now foreigners have control of our jobs, our property and homes.
Please USA, please turn back to Jesus, the Lord of Host.
He will protect this country that we should love the most.
This is my country, this is my home, this is my America.
Help the citizens of this country, to keep it for the people.

William T. Smith

START

Let us start something new
PRAY FOR UNITY
in
AMERICA
While there is still hope
Let us take a stand
Let us start to protect
OUR
Churches from immorality
Let this be the nation
Our forefathers wanted
One nation
Under God
for liberty and justice
for all America

William T. Smith

HOW TO BECOME A CHRISTIAN

By taking three steps, you can make the most important decision of your life---to accept Jesus as your personal Savior and Lord and His gift of forgiveness of your sins.

ADMIT

Admit to God that you are a sinner. Repent, turn away from your sin: For all have sinned, and come short of the glory of God; Romans 3:23. For the wages of sin is death; but the gift of God is eternal life through Jesus Christ our Lord. Romans 6:23. Repent you therefore, and be converted, that your sins may be blotted out, when the times of refreshing shall come from the presence of the Lord; Acts 3:19.

BELIEVE

By faith receive Jesus Christ as God's Son and accept Jesus' gift of forgiveness from sin. For God so loved the world, that he gave his only begotten Son, that whosoever believes in him should not perish, but have everlasting life. John 3:16. Jesus said unto him, I am the way, the truth, and the life; no man comes unto the Father, but by me. John 14:6. Neither is there salvation in any other: for there is none other name under heaven given among men, whereby we must be saved. Acts 4:12. But God commended his love toward us, in that, while we were yet sinners, Christ died for us. Romans 5:8. For by grace are you saved through faith; and that not of yourselves: it is the gift of God: Not of works, lest any man should boast. Ephesians 2:8-9. He came unto his own, and his own received him not. But as many as received him, to them gave he power to become the sons of God, even to them that believe on his name: Which were born, not of blood, nor of the will of the flesh, nor of the will of man,, but of God. John 1:11-13.

CONFESS

Confess your faith in Jesus Christ as Savior and Lord. If we confess our sins, he is faithful and just to forgive us our sins, and to cleanse us from all unrighteousness. I John 1:9. That if you shall confess with your mouth the Lord Jesus, and shall believe in your heart that God has raised him from the dead, you shall be saved. For with the heart man believes unto righteousness; and with the mouth confession is made unto salvation. For whosoever shall call upon the name of the Lord shall be saved. Romans 10:9-10&13.

If you choose right now to believe Jesus died for your sins and receive new life through Him, pray a prayer similar to the one that follows, as you call on Him, and Him alone, to be your Savior and Lord: But pray with an honest heart believing Jesus is your Savior, for He knows if you are sincere or not.

"Dear Heavenly Father, I know I am a sinner and have rebelled against You in many ways. I believe Jesus died for my sin and that only through faith in His death and resurrection can I be forgiven. I now turn from my sin and ask Jesus to come into my life as my Savior and Lord. From this day forward, I will choose to follow Jesus. Thank You, Lord Jesus for loving me and forgiving me. In Jesus' name I pray. Amen."

After you have received Jesus Christ into your life, share your decision with another person. Following Christ's example, ask for baptism by immersion in your local church as a public expression of your faith. Therefore we are buried with him by baptism into death: that like as Christ was raised up from the dead by the glory of the Father, even so we also should walk in newness of life. Romans 6:4. As you have therefore received Christ Jesus the Lord, so walk you in him: Colossians 2:6.

CHAPTER ONE

The United States of America, this is the country I love. But the question is: How much do you love her? Many people love this country for all of the activities a person can do. This country has many beautiful sites and places to go, and do all these things like this thought I have written:

BEAUTIFUL AMERICA

Oh, how beautiful America is from coast to coast.
We have mountains in several states
including Hawaii and Alaska.
These mountains holds many wonders on trails and at resorts.
We have resorts all over this beautiful country of ours.
Places where we can camp, Kayak, fish, or go boating.
Yes: this is a beautiful country, I love this America.
This is also a country with many hunting places in it.
We can hunt deer, elk, rabbit, squirrel, moose and other animals.
We also have race tracks for horses, cars, boats and humans.
Plenty of competition for football, baseball, basketball,
tennis, hockey, skiing, snow boarding,
ice skating and much more.
Yes: this is a beautiful America, a land of the free.
Freedom to go and do any of these different things.
Freedom to live in peace, no matter where we are at.

WILLIAM T. SMITH

There is an old saying, and I like it very much.
Don't treed on my rights, and I won't treed on yours.

William T. Smith

The United States has many interest. If you like the outdoors, we have national parks, zoo's, wildlife conservation, skiing, boating, as well as zoological parks. There are zoo's in every state and in most bigger cities. There are Botanical Gardens and conservancy trails, live volcanoes in different parts of the country. There are also waterfalls, trails and resorts all across this country of ours.

If you like going to the beach and showing off your body; or to just lie in the sun. Maybe play volley ball or just enjoy the outdoors playing in the sand. There are many beaches in America for just that purpose. I am not going to promote any beaches, for there are many of them but I will give you a list of beaches I heard was in the top ten.

Waianapanapa State Park where I hear has several beaches with black sands. Wailea Beach or maybe Kaanapali Beach which I understand are big beaches; and some smaller beaches if you don't like a big one, like Napili Bay Beach or Hookipa Beach Park. All of these plus much more on the island of Maui, but lets not forget the Island of Kauai. There we have Polihale State park, Where there is not only beaches but views that are very beautiful and interesting. As for the beaches there are several to which Ke'e Beach or Tunnels Beach and Hanalei Bay are there. But never forget there are many beaches in the Hawaiian Islands. Now lets go to the east coast of the main land Florida.

Of coarse in Florida there are also some small islands, like Sanibel Island where we have the Lighthouse Beach Park, or the Bowman's Beach, or check out the Tarpon Bay Beach. Then there is the Amelia Island where I hear there are at least 40 different beaches that cover 13 miles. There is also Amelia Island State Park and the Main Beach Park. With these two islands there is a lot to do.

AMERICA, DO WE REALLY LOVE HER?

Being we are talking beaches, we should not forget the mainland Florida where beaches are with different cities. Cities like Naples- Miami Beach- and others, around Naples there is Delnor-Wiggins Pass State Park, and Lowdermilk Park and of course Naples Municipal Beach. Around Miami Beach you will find South Beach and Lummus Park and Haulover Beach Park, where there is much to do.

We are in Florida don't forget Key West the most known island; here we have Zachary Taylor Historic State Park and Smathers Beach. While we are on the east part of the United States I need to check out one more place.

There is an island in North Carolina called Bald Head Island where there is 14 miles of untouched beaches on three sides of this island. These three are called South Beach- North Beach- and East Beach; no matter what the fun is you will find it here. If not there are 200 miles of beaches in North Carolina's Outer Banks. Then Hatteras Island is a good place, as well as Kitty Hawk and Kill Devil Hills. From here lets go to the West Coast of United States main land.

California is where people likes to go, Why, Because just about all of the west coast there are beaches. From California to Oregon there are beaches every where. There is the Cannon Beach in Oregon, you may not be able to swim there for the coast line is very rough. But there is still a lot you can do there. From the North shore line to the South shore line of Monterey we can go to the Point Lobos State Natural Reserve, or the Carmel Beach. If you go up from there you will find Laguna Beach Crescent Bay Beach, Main Beach or Heisler Park.

I know I spent a lot of time on the beaches, but there is a reason, I will let you know later. But in with the beaches we also have many other activities in our country like hiking, visiting National Parks, to visiting theme parks. we have many hiking trails from the east to the west, all the way from Maine to Florida to California to Alaska to Hawaii. Like the Nugget Falls Trail in Alaska; Appalachian Trail in Virginia; Burroughs Mountain Hike in Washington; Halema'uma'u Trail in Hawaii; Charlies

Bunion Hike in Tennessee and North Carolina; Billy Goat Trail in Maryland; Kalalua Trail in Hawaii; Chautauqua Trail in Colorado; Canyon to Rim Loop in Oregon; or the Petroglyph Wall Trail in Nevada.

From what I hear they are all good trails.

We have 63 national parks in the United States, here are some of them: Yellowstone National Park, It covers 2.2 million acres, and covers three different states Wyoming- Montana- and Idaho. Yosemite National Park is in California and two waterfalls and plenty of scenic views. Glacier National Park has 700 lakes and a UNESCO World Heritage Site of Water-Glacier International Peace Park. Grand Canyon is also a UNESCO World Heritage Site, 18 miles wide and 277 miles long, with the Colorado River. This is in the state of Arizona where you probably need a helicopter to see it all.

There is the Grand Teton National Park; that has over 200 miles of trails in Wyoming. But the Bryce Canyon Park in southern Utah has about 35,835 acres that you can do a lot in. If you go to the eastern part of Utah, you will find 77,000 acres of Arches National Park. In Colorado, we have the Rocky Mountain National Park, with 300 miles of trails, and 147 different lakes. We cannot forget the Sequoia National Park in California that has the biggest trees grown. If you like National Parks with all there opportunities.

Then you will love the theme parks that we have- like the Magic Kingdom Park in Orlando, Florida. Or maybe the Universal Islands of Adventure also in Orlando. Or the Disney's Animal Kingdom also in Orlando. The Disney's Hollywood Studios is a great place to go In Orlando. For the last one in Orlando would be Universal Studios Florida. Florida has a lot of recreation, many thing to do, and many places to go and visit. Another one would be Fun Spot America in Kissimmee, Florida.

Let's go to the west coast where we have the Universal Studios Hollywood, in Los Angeles, California. In Anaheim, California we have the Disneyland Park; and the Disney California Adventure Park. But don't leave out the central America. The Dollywood;

AMERICA, DO WE REALLY LOVE HER?

in Pigeon Forge, Tennessee, owned by the singer Dolly Parton. And in Branson, Missouri; we have the Silver Dollar City. There is also the Bay Beach Amusement Park that is located in Green Bay, Wisconsin.

But: I must say that if this is the only reason you love America; It is a Very poor reason. For you can find Activities like these all around this earth. So why do you love this country?

There was a lady named Katharine Lee Bates who wrote a poem; which ladder a man named Samuel A. Ward put music to. This is the poem she wrote:

America, the beautiful

O beautiful for spacious skies, For amber waves of grain.
For purple mountains majesties, Above the fruited plains.
America! America! God shed His grace on thee.
And crown thy good with brotherhood, From sea to shining sea!
O beautiful for pilgrim feet, Whose stern, impassioned stress.
A thorough-fare for freedom beat, Across the wilderness!
America! America! God mend thine every flaw.
Confirm thy soul in self-control, Thy liberty in law!
O beautiful for heroes proved, In liberating strife.
Who more than self their country loved,
And mercy more than life!
America! America! May God thy gold refine.
Till all success be nobleness, and every grain divine!
O beautiful for patriot dream, that sees beyond the years.
Thine alabaster cities gleam, Undimmed by human tears!
America! America! God shed His grace on thee.
And crown thy good with brotherhood, From sea to shining sea.

Katharine Lee Bates

WILLIAM T. SMITH

I have found some quotes from different people about nature:

There is only one earth, and it's the only home we have-- a fact not lost on the untold number of people who have fought to protect the planet and the living creatures on it's surface. Rachel Carson

If men were to be destroyed and the books they have written were to be transmitted to a new race of creatures, in a new world, what kind of record would be found in them of so remarkable a phenomenon as the rainbow? Henry David Thoreau

A grove of giant redwood or sequoias should be kept just as we keep a great and beautiful cathedral. President Theodore Roosevelt

Our planet, the Earth, is, as far as we know, unique in the universe. It contains life. Even in it's most barren stretches, there are animals. Around the equator, where those two essentials for life, sunshine and moisture, are most abundant, great forests grow. And here plants and animals proliferate in such numbers that we still have not named all the different species. David Attenborough

In the woods we return to reason and faith. There I feel that nothing can befall me in life-- no disgrace, no calamity... which nature cannot repair. Ralph Waldo Emerson

Only if we understand can we care. Only if we care will we help. Only if we help shall they be saved.
Jane Goodall

A man on foot, on horseback or on a bicycle will see more, feel more, enjoy more in one mile than a the motorized tourist can in a hundred miles. Edward Abbey

AMERICA, DO WE REALLY LOVE HER?

Acts of creation are ordinarily reserved for gods and poets, but humbler folk may circumvent this restriction if they know how. To plant a pine, for example, one need be neither god or poet: one need only own a good shovel. Aldo Leopold

Let us be the ancestors our descents will thank. Across the continent--- common people with uncommon courage and the whispers of their ancestors in their ears continue their struggles to protect the land and water and trees on which their very existence is based. And lie small tributaries joining together to form a mighty river, their force and power grows. Winona LaDuke

The generation that destroys the environment is not the generation that pays the price. Wangari Maathai

Our goal is not just an environment of clean air and water and scenic beauty. The objective is an environment of decency, quality and mutual respect for all other human beings and all other living creatures. Gaylord Nelson

Within National Parks is room-- glorious room-- room in which to find ourselves, in which to think and hope, to dream and plan, to rest and resolve. Enos Mills

There is nothing so American as our national parks-- The fundamental idea behind the parks-- is that the country belongs to the people, that it is in process of making for the enrichment of the lives of all of us. President Franklin D. Roosevelt

I've been through legislation creating a dozen national parks, and there's always the same pattern. When you first propose a park, and you visit the area and present the case to the local people, they threaten to hang you. You go back in five years and they think it's the greatest thing that ever happened.
Congressman Mo Udall

WILLIAM T. SMITH

National parks are the best idea we ever had. Absolutely American, absolutely democratic, they reflect us at our best rather than our worst. Wallace Stegner

The national parks belong to everyone. To the people. To all of us. The government keeps saying so and maybe, in this one case at least, the government is telling the truth. Hard to believe, but possible.
Edward Abbey

Here is a list of National Parks of the United States; Young Students Learning Library, volume 14; page 1710.

Name	Location	Interesting features
Acadia	Maine	Spectacular wave-battered cliffs, interesting caves, beautiful lakes.
Arches	Utah	Unusual stone arches, windows, pinnacles, and pedestals caused by erosion.
Badlands	South Dakota	Dry area with deep ravines, colorful rocks, fossils.
Big Bend	Texas	Wild animals, Rocky Mountains, Rio Grande.
Biscayne	Florida	Chain of Islands south of Miami.
Bryce Canyon	Utah	14 box canons, magnificent sheer curves of the pink cliffs.
Canyonlands	Utah	Huge mesas, strange rock formations, evidence of prehistoric Indians.
Capitol Reef	Utah	60 mile elevation of sandstone cliffs, highly colored rock, narrow and high gorges.

AMERICA, DO WE REALLY LOVE HER?

Carlsbad Caverns	New Mexico	Fantastic labyrinth under the Guadalupe Mountains.
Channel Islands	California	Sea birds, sea lions, endangered wildlife.
Crater Lake	Oregon	An extinct volcano, Wizard Island, the Phantom Ship.
Denali	Alaska	Name changed from Mt. McKinley National Park--contains highest mountain in the United States.
Everglades	Florida	Mangrove and cypress swamps, rare birds.
Gates of the Arctic	Alaska	Vast north-central wilderness.
Glacier	Montana	60 glaciers and 250 lakes, Going-to-the-Sun Highway.
Glacier Bay	Alaska	Coastal glaciers that move down to the sea.
Grand Canyon	Arizona	Enormous canyon shaped by the Colorado River.
Grand Teton	Wyoming	Breathtaking range of mountains, picturesque lakes.
Great Smokey Mountains	North Carolina and Tennessee	Mountains, forests, lakes, variety of wildlife.
Guadalupe	Texas	McKittrick Canyon open to the public, rest of park Mountains closed.
Haleakala	Hawaii (Mauri Island)	Great dormant volcano.
Hawaii Volcanoes	Hawaii (Hawaii Island)	Active volcanoes, awe-inspiring fire pit.

WILLIAM T. SMITH

Hot Springs	Arkansas	47 hot mineral springs used to treat a number of sicknesses.
Isle Royale	Michigan	Wildlife preserve on a fascinating island in western Lake Superior.
Katmai	Alaska	Valley of Ten Thousand / smokes-volcanic activity.
Kenai Fjords	Alaska	Marine mammals, birdlife abundant.
Kings Canyon	California	Mountains, meadows, forest, lakes, streams, canyons.
Kobuk Valley	Alaska	River is center of the native culture.
Lake Clark	Alaska	Scenic wilderness across Cook Inlet from Anchorage.
Lassen Volcanic	California	Active volcanoes, boiling lakes, lava fields.
Mammoth Cave	Kentucky	Largest single cave in the world.
Mesa Verde	Colorado	Larges cliff dwellings and pueblos in North America.
Mount Rainier	Washington	Extinct volcano with glaciers spreading from its crater.
North Cascades	Washington	Mountains, glaciers, lakes.
Olympic	Washington	Mountains, giant evergreens, flower-drenched meadows, rain forest.
Petrified Forest	Arizona	Forest of petrified wood, prehistoric Indian dwellings.
Redwood	California	Groves of ancient redwood trees along Pacific Coast.
Rocky Mountain	Colorado	Rocky Mountains, lakes, streams, flowers.

AMERICA, DO WE REALLY LOVE HER?

Sequoia	California	Enormous sequoia trees, mountains.
Shenandoah	Virginia	Blue Ridge Mountains, spectacular scenery from Skyline Drive.
Theodore Roosevelt	North Dakota	Little Missouri River valley and T. Roosevelt's ranch.
Virgin Islands	Virgin Islands	Rich tropical vegetation, beaches of beautiful white sand.
Voyageurs	Minnesota	More than 50 lakes, large forests, wildlife.
Wind Cave	South Dakota	Large cavern, Black Hills.
Wrangell-St. Elias	Alaska	Larges area in park system.
Yellowstone	Wyoming Montana Idaho	Canyon, geysers, waterfalls, mountains, petrified forests.
Yosemite	California	Yosemite Valley in Sierra Nevada, waterfalls, beautiful scenery.
Zion	Utah	Canyons, cliffs.

CHAPTER TWO

We call this country a democracy; which means we can do what we want, say what we want and go where we want; as long as what we say, and do, and go does not affect what someone else is saying, doing or going. This is keeping within the laws of this country and the Constitution of this country.

The law states that in any crime committed, we are to consider that person innocent until they are proved guilty. But in todays world, the exact opposite is going on. We believe they are guilty and the courts has to prove their innocence. Also the color of the person puts this into play more and more in this country of today. This started in the late 1900's and early 2000's; where if you are white and arrest a colored you are prejudice against the colored. But if you are colored and arrest a white person than you are prejudice against the white. The law does not discriminate against the color of your skin or of your origin, justice is what the law seeks.

I have seen riots in the streets, and the police are not allowed to protect the citizen or their property. I have seen government officials doing things against the Constitution, and getting away with it. Schools are promoting things that goes against the Constitution, the law of nature and our judges are calling it their right to do so. But: what about the rights of the citizens that does not want these things taught or going on with their children. These are the citizens that are put in contempt of, and given a prison sentence.

AMERICA, DO WE REALLY LOVE HER?

We have many rights in this country. The Bill of Rights at the beginning of the Constitution states this is true. The first ten Amendments are the Bill of Rights ratified in 12/ 15/ 1791; the other seventeen came at a later date. I wrote a thought concerning these rights that we call the Bill of Rights.

BILL OF RIGHTS

Our first right is to have freedom of religion;
It is not to have freedom from religion as claimed.
This freedom also states that we have a place to worship.
It does not say that you can destroy that place for any reason.
We have the freedom of the press to print and to speak.
This right is there for truth and not for persecution of someone.
We have the right to a peaceful assembly gathering.
We can also place a petition on the government to grievance.

Our second right is to be able to bear arms; have a weapon.
This right shall not be infringed on by the government.

Our third right states that we will not be forced to:
Quarter the soldiers in our house in peace or in war.

Our fourth right is the search and seizure of our homes.
We cannot have unreasonable searches without a warrant.
The warrant must describe what to search for and be seized.

Our fifth right is the trail and punishment for citizens..
We cannot be tried twice for the same offense in court.
Nor can a person be a witness against himself in court.
Our sixth right is the right of a speedy trail by witnesses.
We cannot be held for a crime without a speedy trail.

WILLIAM T. SMITH

Our seventh right is to have a trail by jury in civil cases.

Our eighth right is cruel and unusual punishment.
The government cannot punish in excess of the offense.

Our ninth right is the construction of constitution.
The rights of the constitution shall not be denied.

Our tenth right is to elect delegates to the United States.

These are the first; ten rights ratified in 1791.
Times has changed but these rights must stand.
We have amendment of these through-out history.
But the Constitution does not change with ratification.

William T. Smith
From the Constitution

No matter who you are, or what religion you decided to go with; you have the right to pray for our nation. While we are praying for this nation, let us not forget to pray for our leaders. This is the time to pray as the Bible commands us to do.

Honor the King

Honor all men. Love the brotherhood.
Fear (Reverence) God Almighty.
Honor the King or (president and the
elected officers). I Peter 2:17.
It is the glory of God to conceal a thing (not to let it be known).
But the honor of Kings (or Presidents) is
to search out a matter (for truth).

AMERICA, DO WE REALLY LOVE HER?

Search the heavens for height, and search
the earth for depth (for truth).
And the heart of Kings (or Presidents) is
unsearchable. Proverbs 25:2-3.
For rulers are not a terror to good works,
but to the evil (law breakers).
Will you then not be afraid of the power? Do that which is good.
And you shall have praise of the same,
for he is the minister of God.
You do what is evil, be afraid; for he
bears his weapon not in vain.
He is the minister of God, to execute wrath. Romans 13:3-4.
Curse not the King (or President) in your thought (or speech).
Nor curse the rich in your bedroom: Ecclesiastes 10:20.
Offer sacrifices of sweet savors unto God of heaven;
And pray for the life of the King (or
President) and his sons. Ezra 6:10.
In the multitude of people is the king's (or President's) honor.
The want of the people is the destruction
(fall of the nation) Proverbs 14:28.
Now you are the body of Christ, and members in Particular.
God has set some in the church, first apostles,
second prophets, third teachers,
After that miracles, then gift of healing, helps, GOVERNMENT:
Diversities of tongues (other languages). I Corinthians 12:27-28.
God respects government: Kings and Presidents; so should you.

William T. Smith

All of this is in keeping with the law of God: Let every soul be subject unto the higher powers. For there is no power but of God: the powers that be ordained of God. Whosoever therefore resist the power, resist the ordinance of God: and they that resist shall receive to themselves damnation.

For rulers are not a terror to good works, but to evil. Will you then not be afraid of the power? Do that which is good, and you shall have praise of the same: For he is the minister of God to you for good. But if you do that which is evil, be afraid; for he bears not the sword in vain: for he is the minister of God, a revenger to execute wrath upon him that does evil.

Wherefore you must need to be subject, not only for wrath, but also for conscience sake. For this cause you pay tribute also: for they are God's ministers, attending continually upon this very thing. Render therefore to all their dues: tribute to whom tribute is due; custom to whom custom is due; reverence to whom reverence is due; honor to whom honor is due. Romans 13:1-7.

Having said this; we should pray for our leaders and for our country. I wrote this about praying.

Pray for those in Authority

I strongly advice you that you pray
earnestly for our President daily.
First of all supplication, intercessions,
and giving thanks day by day.
Pray for all people, especially Kings,
Presidents and those in authority.
That we may lead a quiet and peaceful
life, in this country and world.
With all honesty and glory that leads to
all godliness, in Christ Jesus.
In doing so we may be acceptable unto
Jesus our Lord and Savior.
We do this with faith and a good
conscience; to glorify Christ Jesus.
As we pray to Jesus, our Spiritual King we
should also pray for our President.
For there is only one God, and one mediator
between God and mankind.

AMERICA, DO WE REALLY LOVE HER?

There is only one President, and many
leaders in this country of ours.
Therefore we pray for President and all
Federal and State authorities.
Including Governors and all his staff and
those we have elected to serve.
In doing so; we honor all our elected
personal in State and Country.
We also honor the Lord God of heaven
and earth in spirit and truth.

William T. Smith

As we are praying for our leaders, there comes a time that the leaders needs to step down and let someone else take over. In those times we go to the voting poles and vote for who we believe would be the best candidate. The constitution declares that we have a right to vote, but not everybody can vote, that is why I wrote this on voting.

VOTING IN THE USA

A citizen is one born in the United States of America.
A citizen is one that is naturalized in the United States.
A citizen can vote in every and all elections that is held.
A citizen can vote without being denied or abridged.
A citizen will not be prevented from voting in elections.
Nor will not be prevented because of race, color, or servitude.
A citizen can vote no matter of sex, race or color.
A citizen can vote when he or she becomes eighteen.
Who then cannot vote: Is one that is an alien, or illegal.

WILLIAM T. SMITH

You cannot vote if you are deceased or declared incompetent.
You cannot vote if you are under the age of eighteen.
You cannot vote more than one time in any election.

Amendments 14 – 15 – 19 – 26.

William T. Smith

    We should serve our country in what ever place we can. When we represent our country, we are doing God's will, as long as we do it honestly. When we make laws that goes against our Constitution then we must do what Peter said, When the officials told him this: Did not we straitly command you that you should not teach in Jesus' name? And, behold, you have filled our streets with your doctrine, and intend to bring this Jesus' blood upon us. Then Peter and the other apostles answered and said, We ought to obey God rather than man. So when you are making the laws, do not stray from the Constitution that was ratified.
    In speaking of making laws for this country, I think we also should look at how and why and who are responsible for these laws. So I wrote this with the seven articles that I was reading from our Constitution:

THE CONSTITUTION OF THE USA.
SEVEN ARTICLES

The preamble of the Constitution of
the United States of America.
We the people of the United Stated; that means you the citizen.
In order to form a more perfect Union:
better than what they had.
Establish Justice, insure domestic tranquility:
justifiable laws for peace.
Provide for the common defense: able to defend from terrorism.

AMERICA, DO WE REALLY LOVE HER?

Promote the general Welfare: make sure
the citizens are protected.
And secure the Blessings of Liberty:
being free to make decisions.
To ourselves and our Posterity: work and
invest in our life and country.
Do ordain and establish this Constitution for the United States.
We will do what is necessary to keep
our nation free for the people.
This preamble is the start of what the Constitution is all about.
We have seven articles for this to be the
best country in the world.

Article one: The Legislative Branch- with ten sections.
The Legislature- the House- the Senate- Elections- Meetings-
Membership- Rules- Journals- Adjournments- Compensation-
Revenue Bills- Legislative Process- Presidential Veto- Power
of Congress- limits on congress- Powers prohibited of States.

Article two: The Executive Branch- with four sections.
The President- Civilian Power over Military- Cabinet- Pardon
Power- Appointments- State of the
Union- Convening Congress-
Disqualification.

Article three: The Judicial Branch- with three sections.
Judicial powers- Trail by jury- Original Jurisdiction- Jury trails-
Treason.

Article four: The States- with four sections.
Each State to Honor all others- State citizens- Extradition-
New States- Republican government.

Article five: Amendment- no sections.

Article six: Debts- Supremacy- Oaths- no sections.

WILLIAM T. SMITH

Article seven: Ratification- no sections.

William T. Smith
Taken from the Constitution

After reading these Articles, I remembered what Jesus said about taxes owed to the government. And they send unto Jesus certain of the Pharisees and of the Herodians, to catch Jesus in his words. And when they were come, they said unto him, Master, we know that you are true, and cares for no man: for you regarded not the person of men, but teaches the way of God in truth: Is it lawful to give taxes to Caesar, or not? Shall we give, or shall we not give? But Jesus, knowing their hypocrisy, said unto them, Why tempt you me? Bring me a penny, that I may see it. And they brought it. And Jesus

said unto them, Whose is this image and superscription? And they said unto Jesus, Caesar's. And Jesus answering said unto them, Render to Caesar the things that are Caesar's, and to God the things that are God's. And they marveled at Jesus. Mark 12:13-17. Where this thought came to mind.

Federal Tax Payers

The IRS is a dreaded name in the United States of America.
In reality only those who are avoiding
paying taxes should worry.
You are a hard working citizen, having taxes paid from earning.
Then you have nothing to worry about
the IRS; they are not after you.
There was one year that I missed
calculated my taxes, got a letter.
The IRS sent me a letter first, I had to call then on a certain day.

AMERICA, DO WE REALLY LOVE HER?

When I called, we talked and the IRS
told me the problem on my tax.
After hearing what they said, I made a
deal to pay them my under taxes.
I was not penalized because of the mistake
that was made. You ask why?
I did not do it deliberately; and made
arrangement to pay what I owed.
I did what the Bible said. I paid USA what
I owed, I paid God what I owed.

William T. Smith

I wrote another one about State taxes here in Illinois.

Illinois Tax Payers

In Illinois: the taxes are being raised for unnecessary things.
The people are leaving because they wish not to pay for them.
The last two or so Governors of this State of Illinois was bad.
Not keeping their promise they made to our citizens here.
Our tax dollars are being spent on the whelms of rich citizens.
Those that have the money to pay off the Governors it seems.
These projects should have been voted on in the election.
But: instead were approved by unlawful means of government.
But putting aside these issues, the tax raise is causing lay-offs.
Companies are laying off, because they to are getting hit hard.
How can we make this State self- efficient, doing it that way.
Companies cannot pay workers; Workers cannot pay taxes.
Governor wake-up and look at what you are doing to Illinois.
If the people cannot work; How are they going to live and eat?
One way, is to raise more taxes; to house
and feed the unemployed.
So how is this helping the state of Illinois?
I cannot find it this way!

WILLIAM T. SMITH

Put people to work, then you can cut the
taxes; do not add more debt.

William T. Smith

In 1831 a man named Samuel F. Smith wrote a hymn that Thesaurus Musicus put to music.

My Country, 'Tis of Thee

My country 'tis of thee, Sweet land of liberty, of Thee I sing:
Land where my fathers died, Land of the pilgrims, pride,
From every mountain side Let freedom ring!
My native country, thee, Land of the noble free, thy name I love:
I love Thy rocks and rills, Thy woods and templed hills;
My heart with rapture thrills Like that above.
Let music swell the breeze, And ring from all the trees
Sweet freedom's song: Let mortal tongues
awake;Let all that breathe
partake; Let rocks there silence break, The sound prolong.
Our fathers' God, to thee, Author of liberty, To Thee we sing:
Long may our land be bright With freedom's holy light;
Protect us by Thy might, Great God our King!

Samuel F. Smith

Another great song by Francis Scott Key in 1814 tells it all.

The Star-Spangled Banner

O say, can you see, by the dawn's early light,
What so proudly we hailed at the twilight's last gleaming.
O say, does that star-spangled banner yet wave
O'er the land of the free and home of the brave?

AMERICA, DO WE REALLY LOVE HER?

In a Presidential Address; President Ronald Reagan said: "Freedom prospers when religion is vibrant and the rule of the law under God is acknowledged" that was is March 8, 1983. So what has happened to this nation that used to believe in the Supreme Being of God Almighty? President Reagan also went on to say: "The real crisis we face today is a spiritual one; at root, it is a test of moral will and faith."

President Abraham Lincoln once prayed this prayer: "I believe in Him whose will, not ours, is done."

"I believe I am a humble instrument in the hand of our Heavenly Father." "If we do not do right I believe God will let us go our own way to ruin. But if we do right, I believe He will lead us safely out of this wilderness, adorning our arms with victory."

And you shall know the truth, and the truth shall make you free. John 8-32. What kind of freedom was Jesus talking about here? Here's the answer: Jesus answered them; Verily, verily, I say unto you, Whosoever commits sin is the servant of sin. And the servant abides not in the house forever: but the son abides ever. If the Son therefore shall make you free, you shall be free indeed. John 8:34-36. If you do not have this freedom then you are not free and your father is the devil, and the lust of your father will you do. What are the lust of your father the devil? Here is a small list of things that are mentioned!

And being you did not like to retain God in your knowledge, God gave you over to a reprobate mind, to do those things which are not convenient: Being filled with all unrighteousness, fornication, wickedness, covetousness, maliciousness; full of envy, murder, debate, deceit, malignity; whisperers, backbiters, haters of God and the Godhead, despiteful, proud, boasters inventors of evil things, disobedient to parents, without understanding, covenant breakers, without natural affection, implacable, unmerciful, adultery, uncleanness, lasciviousness, idolatry, witchcraft, hatred, variance, emulations, wrath, strife, seditions, heresies, drunkenness, revealings, and such like. Knowing the judgment of God, that they that commit such things are worthy of death. Not only you, but who takes pleasure in or helps those watching you do them. Therefore you are inexcusable, and you shall be judged! As it is written they that do such things shall not inherit the kingdom of God. Romans 1:28-2:1, and Galatians 5:19-21.

I received this in the mail, and I do not think they would mind if I passed it on to all of you.

DECLARATION of DEPENDENCE UPON GOD AND HIS HOLY BIBLE

We hold these truths to be self-evident, that all men are created equal and endowed by their Creator with certain unalienable rights. Since our Creator gave us these rights, we declare that no government has the right to take them away. Among these rights is the right to exercise our Christian beliefs as put forth in God's Holy Bible.

We therefore declare that God grants life at conception and no one has the right to take that life unless it is a direct threat to the life of the mother.

Marriage was instituted by God between one man and one woman. The Lord gave only this family unit the responsibility to have children and raise them in the fear of the Lord.

We therefore respectfully reserve the right to refuse any mandate by the government that forces us to fund or support abortion. We also oppose same-sex marriage, polygamy, bestiality, and all other forms of sexual perversion prohibited by Holy Scripture.

We proclaim that Jesus has provided the cure for all sin and therefore reach out to the sinner in love, but do not embrace the sin, knowing its destructive nature.

Therefore, we, the undersigned- not only as Christians but also believing we have the constitutional right as Americans to

AMERICA, DO WE REALLY LOVE HER?

follow these time honored Christian beliefs- commit to conducting our churches, ministries, businesses, and personal lives in accordance with our Christian faith and choose to obey God rather than man.

www.DependenceOnGod.com

CHAPTER THREE

Down through history men have fought and died to keep this country free. As long as we have people in this world that wants more and more; we will have wars. Some times these wars works on who we are and our morality go way down; but we must keep faith in our Lord, Jesus Christ. With this thought in mind I wrote this thought:

Our Moral Standard

Morality is a doctrine or system of moral conduct.
It is also a particular moral principles of moral teaching.
All of this is conforming to ideals of right human conduct.
In this we lift the morale of the people our citizens.
So that the ethics and the virtue keeps the spirits high.
But is this the message we are sending to our children today.
The government is trying to take over the churches.
When that happens our church will be like our schools.
The schools teach many things that are not of moral state.
Things like sex education with more than one sexual identity.
Like abortion is not the murder of our unborn citizens.
Printing money with no capital behind what is printed.
The moral standard in America is so low, all we see is dirt.
If we want high morals in this country? Turn to Christ Jesus!!!

William T. Smith

AMERICA, DO WE REALLY LOVE HER?

When we keep our morals up then great things will happen. To keep our morals up we must belong to God; Jesus in us will bring out God's morals in us.

A LIFE LAID DOWN

We owe a debt to the United States of America's military for their courageous service. The greatest thing a person can give is his life. There have been millions of soldiers who have laid down their lives for the freedom and safety of our country. Just as soldiers have given their lives for America, so Jesus Christ laid down His life for the world.

1) A LIFE IN DANGER

Every day soldiers put their lives in danger for our freedom. Yet more dangerous than losing a life is losing a soul. All mankind is in danger of death and Hell because of sin. "For all have sinned, and come short of the glory of God." Romans 3:23. Man came short of Heaven (the glory of God) because of sin! Not only does sin keep a person out of Heaven, but it also condemns a person to Hell. Romans 6:23 says, "For the wages of sin is death;.." Sin brings both physical and spiritual death. "And death and Hell were cast into the lake of fire. This is the second death." Revelation 20:14.

2) A LIFE LAID DOWN

A soldier willingly gives his life for his family, his fellow soldiers, and his country, yet Jesus Christ willingly gave His life for the world. I Corinthians 15:3 says, "... Christ died for our sins according to the scriptures;" His death, burial, and resurrection provided the only way for man to go to heaven. "But God commendeth his love toward us,, in that, while we were yet sinners, Christ died for us." Romans 5:8. Jesus sacrificed His life so all could live!

WILLIAM T. SMITH

3) A LIFE SAVED

A soldier's obedience to training and orders will determine life or death on the battlefield, Likewise, man determines his eternal life of eternal death by what he does with God's orders. God's orders are simple; all must repent and believe. Acts 20:21 says, "...Repentance toward God, and faith toward our Lord Jesus Christ."

To save your life, you must now receive Christ by calling on Him in prayer. Romans 10:13 says, "For whosoever shall call upon the name of the Lord shall be a saved." When you say this prayer, say it with faith believing, and with an honest heart. For God knows if you really mean it or out; so be honest with yourself as well as with God.

Let us Pray: Dear Lord Jesus, I know that I am a sinner, please forgive me of my sin, and take me to Heaven when I die. I believe that You died and rose again for me. I am trusting You completely and nothing I can do on earth for your salvation will save me but Your grace and mercy. Thank You Jesus for dieing for me! Amen.

Mercy and Truth Ministries
Lawrence Kansas USA

I wrote this thought knowing that a soldier will lay down his life for his country; in doing this he does keep freedom in force for the citizens that cannot or will not go to war. Likewise Jesus laid down His life for the mankind, even though mankind deserves death for the sin and shame that he does. Jesus loves mankind that much; just as a soldier loves his country and will die for it, in order for all citizens can be free. Jesus wants all mankind to be free, that is why He came to the earth and die on a cross being innocent of any crime. All you have to do is believe and sin no more, it does not mean that you can willing sin because Jesus forgave you.

AMERICA, DO WE REALLY LOVE HER?

Great Things

All the great things we know, are simple.
And can be expressed in a single word:
Freedom- Justice- Duty- Mercy- Hope.
Winston Churchhill made this quote:
Freedom: being independent in liberty.
Justice: the establishment of rights.
Duty: a moral obligation to parents and country.
Mercy: showing kindness and goodwill.
Hope: a desire for expecting the impossible.
I think some other words should be added.
Like maybe these: Trust- Service- Faith:
Trust: to place confidence in someone.
Service: being able to help when needed.
Faith: belief and trust and loyalty.
If you have these eight on your mind.
Then great things will begin to happen.

William T. Smith

We are serving our country in many different ways. Some of us will serve in the military. The Army- Navy- Marines- Air force- Coast guard- or Border patrol; And we usually forget those on the front lines here at home. The local Police- County Police- State Police- Home Security- FBI- and like it or not; our politicians. All of these are fighting for our freedoms, we can not be free if we are not willing to fight for what we believe in.

Freedom is Duty

Freedom consists not in doing what we like,
But in having the right to do what we ought. Pope John Paul II.
One thing about freedom is being frank, open and outspoken.
That is known as the freedom of speech in the Constitution.

WILLIAM T. SMITH

Freedom is a privilege that is yours as a citizen of America.
Freedom is a liberty to have what you can afford in life.
This freedom does have some limits, getting licenses for things.
If you wish to drive, you are free to get a drivers license.
If you wish to hunt, you are free to get a hunting license.
That goes for fishing, or any other sport, or owning a business.
With all of this, then we can do what we ought to do.
That is a moral obligation to do what we know is right.
Come to think of it, it is not just an obligation, but a duty.
It is our duty to pay taxes, and take care of our family.
In saying this, it is not only our right to go to church.
But it is also our obligation to keep the building in good shape.
It is our duty to pay tithes and to support
the pastor of that church.
So: is it our duty to live our life like Jesus did here on earth.
When we accept Jesus as our Lord- Savior- Redeemer- King;
We not only have that duty, but have that privilege to serve Him.

William T. Smith

And speaking of serving; we must also serve and protect this nation and the freedoms it gives to us.

In order to protect we must also have to fight. There are those that want to take these freedoms from us; when this happens, we must fight, whereby I wrote this thought:

FIGHTING FOR AMERICA

We grow-up with the right to serve in the armed forces.
This can be Army, Navy, Marines, Coast Guard, Air Force.
We are called to defend, protect and even die for freedom.
This is not just a right, but it is more of a privilege.
It should be our privilege, as well as a duty to do so.
I was in the draft during the Vietnam war, and appeared.
But: for some reason or another, I was never called.

AMERICA, DO WE REALLY LOVE HER?

My desire at that time was to go and fight where needed.
I know of many people some in my own family that did.
Some of them never came back from the war they fought.
Some of them came back from war, only to get killed.
The police and fire departments is also warriors of USA.

William T. Smith

We do have what is own as conscientious objectors; these are people who refuses to serve in the armed forces or to bear arms on the grounds of moral or religious principles. When these people has to make a decision to serve in a war; they come into a conflict with themselves and what they believe. In thinking about this, I was watching a television show called (Magnum P.I.) where I heard a statement, that brought about this thought:

IN CONFLICT

Why do you always put me in conflict with myself?
A question that Tom Selleck asked on Magnum P.I..
This is what happens every time you read or study the Bible
For the pages of the Bible comes alive and will condemn you.
For this reason, God sent his son Jesus to redeem the earth.
With Adam and Eve, we all fall short and are now sinners.
With Jesus, God's Son, we all can be forgiven of these sins.
When we ask for forgiveness of Jesus, he will forgive you.
For Jesus did not come to the earth to destroy the sinner.
But that the sinner could have eternal life in Christ Jesus.
For dust we were made, and unto dust shall this body return.
We will receive a new body, where we can look upon God.
This new body will ether have eternal life with Christ Jesus.
Or, this new body will have eternal death without God our hope.
The choice is up to you, while you are living on this earth.
Chose wisely and live; or, chose poorly and have eternal death.
Eternal life with Jesus in glory, or as some people say, in heaven.

WILLIAM T. SMITH

Eternal death without God or hope, as
some say is hell or torment.

William T. Smith

It was during one of these wars to protect our nation when the birth of our National Anthem came to light. The war of 1812 is where the White House and the Capitol Building and the Library of Congress was burnt to the ground. A man named Francis Scott Key was aboard the enemy ship when he wrote these words, that is now our National Anthem.

The Defense of Fort McHenry

O say, can you see, by the dawn's early light
What so proudly we hail at the twilight's last gleaming
Whose broad stripes and bright stars, through the perilous fight
Over the ramparts we watched, were so gallantly streaming?
And the rockets' red glare, the bombs bursting in air
Gave proof through the night that our flag was still there.
O say, does that Star-spangled Banner Yet wave
Over the land of the free and the home of the brave?
O thus be it ever when free men shall stand
Between their loved homes and the war's desolation
Blest with victory and peace, may the heaven rescued land
Praise the power that hath made and preserved us a nation!
Then conquer we must, when our cause it is just
And this be our motto: "In God is our trust!"
And the Star-spangled Banner in triumph shall wave
Over the land of the free and home of the brave.

Francis Scott Key

This poem became our National Anthem in 1931, and the name of this poem was changed to "The Star-Spangled Banner". I for one believes that this title is well deserved: Thank you Francis

AMERICA, DO WE REALLY LOVE HER?

Scott Key for this great poem, which was put to music, Thank you who ever you are for the music.

I would like to put in a prayer that was put into a song by Edward Hughes Pruden in 1952. The music for this prayer came from a Netherlands Folk Song, I believed called Kremser back in 1626.

O GOD OF OUR FATHERS

O God of our fathers, we praise and adore thee
For all thy great mercies through years that are gone
Thy guidance and goodness through many generations
Have brought us now at last to a new day's bright dawn.
Help us to be faithful to thee and thy kingdom
Thy church, and the work of our Christ in all lands
May loyalty, sacrifice, courage now attend us
And bring to fullest triumph thy work in our hands.
Our task is no greater than that which our fathers
Assumed with fidelity, courage and pride
We know that all mountains will vanish now before us
If thou wilt point the way and remain at our side.
We now reaffirm our undying devotion
We pray thou wilt fill us with all strength and grace
Crown all high endeavors with victories forever
And may we run with faithfulness life's fateful race.
A-men

Edward Hughes Pruden

If you have noticed with all of this, we must fight; in order to fight we need weapons and know how to use them. The government down through our history promoted the use of weapons and that private citizens should bear arms. These citizens should also be ready to fight for the country we live in. The second Amendment has this clause printed into the constitution just for that purpose; It reads:

WILLIAM T. SMITH

A well regulated Militia, being necessary to the security of a free state, the right of the people to keep and bear Arms, shall not be infringed. U. S. Constitution- 2nd Amendment.

Even some of our Presidents made speeches concerning this issue. Here are some of there quotes:

" A free people ought not only to be armed, but disciplined to which end a uniform and well-digested plan is requisite; and their safety and interest require that they should promote such manufactories …."
President George Washington

"Arms in the hands of the citizens maybe used at individual discretion for defense of the country, the overthrow of tyranny, or private self-defense"
President John Adams

"No freeman shall be debarred the use of arms within his own lands.
President Thomas Jefferson

"An efficient militia is authorized and contemplated by the Constitution and required by the spirit and safety of the free government."
President James Madison

"A million armed freemen, possessed of the means of war, can never by conquered by a foreign foe."
President Andrew Jackson

" The people of these United States are the rightful masters of both congress and courts, not to over-throw the Constitution, but to over-throw the men who pervert that Constitution."
President Abraham Lincoln

AMERICA, DO WE REALLY LOVE HER?

"Let us speak courteously, deal fairly, and keep ourselves armed and ready."

President Teddy Roosevelt

"Today, we need a nation of Minutemen.... who regard the preservation of freedom as the basic purpose of their daily life and who are willing to consciously work and sacrifice for that freedom."

President John F. Kennedy

"Self defense is not our right, it is our duty."

President Ronald Reagan

"We will defend privacy, free speech, religious liberty, and the right to keep and bear arms."

President Donald Trump

This came from a letter from the American Mint. Thanks for these writings.

The government now wants to abolish these rights that we have, because they are letting people into our country that does not have respect for our country or the citizens living in our country. This brings into play a lot of violence and the government wants to punish the citizens of this country for something that they caused in the first place. Whereby I wrote this thought:

THERE IS NO PEACE

Peace: A state of tranquility or quiet; harmony.
Destruction comes; and they shall seek peace, but
There shall be none, for we cry for peace and see war.
We looked for peace, but no good came for a time.
Behold the trouble that comes when Kings want more.
They have healed the hurt of the people slightly, saying

WILLIAM T. SMITH

Peace, peace; when there is no peace to be had.
As it is written, there is none righteous, no, not one.
There is none that understands, there is none that seek God.
Destruction and misery are in their ways; all their days.
There is no fear of God before their eyes; only evil, evil, evil.
And the way of peace have they not known, only destruction.
There is no judgment in their goings, their paths are crooked.
Whoever goes with them, shall never know peace, no never.
Destruction comes, and they shall seek
peace, there will be none.
Now the end has come upon them, and God will send his anger.
He will judge them according to their ways, and evil acts.
There will be recompense upon them in all their abominations.

William T. Smith

This also means that perilous times are coming our way. Will we be able to overcome all of this trouble that our leaders are bringing upon this country. We will if only we turn back to what our forefathers wanted for this country. Here is a thought I have on this subject:

PERILOUS TIMES

It is written that in the last days perilous times will come.
This is some of the things that will happen at that time.
Men shall be lovers of their own selves; II Timothy 3.
This means that people will do their own thing; not God's.
Covetous, boasters, proud, blasphemers, unthankful people.
All of these states that these people should never be trusted.
Disobedient to parents, unholy, without natural affection.
This means that they are unruly and being homosexual.
Truce breakers, false accusers, incontinent, fierce sort of crowd.
This means they are a lier and will do anything for themselves.
Despiser of those that are good, traitors, heady, high-minded.

AMERICA, DO WE REALLY LOVE HER?

> We see this in all the churches being
> burned, the good people in jail.
> Lovers of pleasure more than lovers of God. II Timothy 3:1-4.
> People would rather go to a ballgame or race instead of church.
> Having a form of godliness, but denying the power thereof.
> These are people to shun or stay away from, turn away.
>
> William T. Smith

So America, Do you really love her; or do you just love the thought that you are free?

This is a question that only you can answer, for you know your heart.

Are you willing to abide by the Constitution of the United States of America?

Are you willing to fight for your country, even if fighting means death?

Are you going to let others have their opinion when it differs from yours?

There are many religions within our borders today. The Constitution is there for your right to worship the God or gods of your choice. In doing so you are protected by law and the Constitution, but remember so are the other religions around you.

The religion of your choice is protected by law.

The right to bear arms is protected by law.

You have the right to do anything you wish; remember so does the other person.

If you love America; prove it by obeying the laws of this country!

If you love America; prove it by obeying the Constitution of America.

WILLIAM T. SMITH

What I have been seeing here lately, does not show me that you love America!

It shows me that you love yourself more than you love this country of freedom!

This country is made of immigrants from the beginning; Immigrants are a plus to this nation of America. We welcome all immigrants to this country, but please be legal about coming to the United States of America. And by all means learn the language so we can communicate; also our laws so that you can and will live in peace and let others do the same.

I love this country of United States of America. I have the freedom to go and do what ever I please; as long as I don't keep someone else from that same freedom. When that happens then I will lose the freedom I hold so dear to me; and will land up behind bars in a prison somewhere.

This is my last appeal for you to accept the freedom of this country, but also the freedom that comes with accepting Jesus as your Lord.

Submit yourselves to every ordinance of man for the Lord's sake: whether it be to the King or President, as supreme; or unto governors, as unto them that are sent by him for the punishment of evildoers, and for the praise of them that do well. For so is the will of God, that with well doing you may put to silence the ignorance of foolish men: As free, and not using your liberty for a coat of maliciousness, but as the servant of God. Honor all men. Love the brotherhood. Reverence God. Honor the King or President. I Peter 2:13-17.

Let no corrupt communication proceed out of your mouth, but that which is good to the use of edifying, that it may minister grace unto the hearers. Ephesians 4:29.

And live at peace with one another.

AMERICA, DO WE REALLY LOVE HER?

This is the form of Government that we have and want to protect:

CONSTITUTION

Legislative	Judicial
Senate President House of Representatives	Supreme Court and lower courts as specified in the constitution

Executive office	Cabinet Departments	
Bureau of the Budget The White House Office National Security Council (includes C. I. A.) Council of Economic Advisers Office of Defense Mobilization	State Treasury Defense Justice Interior	Agriculture Commerce Labor Post Office Health, Education and Welfare

SOME IMPORTANT INDEPENDENT FEDERAL AGENCIES

ACTION- Controls programs for aid to needy areas at home and abroad. It administers Vista and Peace corps organizations.
Central Intelligence 'agency- Is responsible for the intelligence operations of the United States government.
Consumer Product Safety Commission- Establishes safety standards for consumer products and bans dangerous products.
Environmental Protection Agency- Leads the government's fight against pollution.

WILLIAM T. SMITH

Equal Employment Opportunity Commission- Is responsible for the prevention of discrimination in employment.

Export-Import Bank of the United States- Provides aid in financing exports and imports of commodities.

Federal Communications Commission- Licenses broadcast stations and regulates some aspects of the programming of broadcasts stations as a whole.

Federal Deposit Insurance Corporation- Insures the deposits of most banks in the United States.

Federal Election Commission- Controls distribution of public funds for federal elections and checks compliance with Federal Election Campaign Act.

Federal Maritime Commission- Administers federal laws relating to United States shipping operations.

Federal Reserve System- Influences the flow of credit and money in the United States.

Federal Trade Commission- Attempts to keep business fair and competitive.

General Accounting Office- Examines the accounts of most federal agencies and provides
congress with reports.

General Services Administration- Manages federal property.

Government Printing Office- Is responsible for government publications.

International Communications Agency- Provides information to foreign countries about the United States and conducts cultural exchange programs.

Interstate Commerce Commission- Enforces federal laws concerning transportation of people or property across state lines.

Library of Congress- Provides research and other materials to Congress and members of the public.

National Aeronautics and Space Administration- Develops, constructs, tests, and operates manned and unmanned vehicles used in the exploration of space.

AMERICA, DO WE REALLY LOVE HER?

National Foundation on Arts and the Humanities- Provides financial and other assistance to the arts and humanities.
National Labor Relations Board- Prevents unfair labor practices by either unions or employers.
National Science Foundation- Supports research in science by awarding grants to qualified individuals and institutions.
Nuclear Regulatory Commission- Licenses and regulates the uses of nuclear energy.
Office of Personnel Management- Checks competency of applicants for jobs in competitive service and classifies jobs.
Securities and exchange Commission- Enforces federal laws concerning the purchase and sale of securities.
Selective Service System- Is responsible for providing enough personnel for the Armed Forces.
Small Business Administration- Tries to help small businesses by use of loans and government contracts.
Tennessee Valley Authority- Is responsible for the development of resources in the Tennessee Valley.
Veterans Administration- Administers laws concerning benefits for men who served in the Armed Forces.

This is not a complete list of agencies in the Federal Government, but as you read through these, you probably noticed that the people that runs these agencies are not doing their job. I don't have to point them out, for you should recognize where they are slipping. I still think we need some of these agencies, but I also think they need to be working for the people of the United States instead of just a few citizens that want federal jobs. We do elect the one that create these jobs, let them regulate the agency with fairness of all the citizens.

WILLIAM T. SMITH

STEPS TO GOD

SEEK:
Seek the Lord while he may be found; call on him while he is near. Isaiah 55:6.

CONFESS:
Then I acknowledged my sin to you and did not cover up my iniquity. I said, "I will confess my transgressions to the LORD"-- and you forgave the guilt of my sin. Psalm 32:5.

HEAR:
I tell you the truth, whoever hears my words and believes him who sent me has eternal life and will not be condemned; he has crossed over from death to life. John 5:24.

BELIEVE:
Believe in the Lord Jesus, and you will be saved--- you and your household. Acts 16:31.

And without faith it is impossible to please God, because anyone who comes to him must earnestly seek him. Hebrews 11:6.

OBEY:
Not everyone who says to me, "Lord, Lord," will enter the kingdom of heaven, but only he who does the will of my Father who is in heaven. Matthew 7:21.

COME:
Come to me, all you who are weary and burdened, and I will give you rest. Matthew 11:28.

RECEIVE:
Yet to all who receive him, to those who believe in his name, he gave the right to become children of God. John 1:12.

BE BAPTIZED:
And now what are you waiting for? Get up, be baptized and wash your sins away, calling on his name. Acts 22:16.

PRAY:
Everyone who calls on the name of the Lord will be saved. Romans 10:13.

AMERICA, DO WE REALLY LOVE HER?

FOLLOW:
Jesus said, "I am the light of the world. Whoever follows me will never walk in darkness, but will have the light of life." John 8:12.

SOW:
Do not be deceived: God cannot be mocked. A man reaps what he sows. The one who sows to please his sinful nature, from that nature will reap destruction; the one who sows to please the Spirit, from the Spirit will reap eternal life. Galatians 6:7-8.

If you are ready to take these steps to God, pray a prayer similar to this a believing and honest heart:

"Lord, Jesus, I believe that you died to pay for my sins. I want you to be Lord of my life. Please come into my heart so I may follow you. Amen"

Let a pastor or another Christian know what you did. Then go to a Bible believing church and get baptized and join the church. After that read your Bible daily and always ask Jesus to give you understanding of his Word.

CHAPTER FOUR

The Congregation

Our churches are full, but the word of God is not preached.
The ministers are tickling the ears of the congregation today.
The congregation is saying, the Lord has saved us from evil.
So we can do these things and not have evil come upon us.
Nor shall famine or the sword of God come upon us this day.
The ministers of God are telling us to repent from this evil.
But the evil is getting stronger and stronger everyday we live.
Therefore your eyes are not upon the truth of our Lord Jesus.
Your loved ones get sick and die, your grief has consumed them.
No! they have made their faces hard as a rock against the Lord;
And still do not call upon the Lord Jesus for their salvation.
You! The people of this nation have done two great evils here.
We are against the Creator God who
made this earth and heaven.
First: we have forgotten the Lord who
is the fountain of living water.
Second: we have dug wells that are dry,
and will not hold the Spirit.
I say this for the wickedness of this nation
has grown out of bounds.
This nation does not reverence the Lord
God any more like it should.
We say there is no God, and we worship the gods of this earth.

AMERICA, DO WE REALLY LOVE HER?

These gods that prevail nothing we want,
and not the God of Creation.
The pastors and the evangelist are
transgressing against God Almighty.
And having the people to believe that they
can do whatever they please.
And still be in the glory of God Almighty
with all these evil things.
Wake-up America and start living right
as the Lord Jesus declares us.
Repent of your sin and your shortcomings,
and serve the Lord God.

William T. Smith

Our forefathers did not set this nation up so that we would forget the Lord God; but that we would glory in the works that God showed us. Look at what our forefathers went through and what they overcame, just because they believed in a God that would help them to overcome the enemy. We see the enemy of today, and we crawl under our tables and hide in our closets, so that we will not face and overcome the evil that is already here.

We have not corrected our children, and now our children are doing abominable things, and not knowing what sex they were born with. The sad part is, we are still not correcting them, nor do we show love toward our children, as we let the government also turn a blind eye to this horrifying situation. It seems like this is the movement of our country; being that our elected officials are just as perverted and corrupt and ungodly as they want our citizens to be.

We murder our unborn children and some pastors, or their wifes get up and says it felt good to do this evil thing. I was appalled when I first heard of a female pastor proclaiming this very thing. What has the churches came to, when we say Lord; Lord and do not the commandments that was laid out for a child of God. We are teaching that which the world is teaching, and not what the Bible has to say about these subjects.

How long shall we commit adultery with other religions and still say we are a Christian nation. No! We are not obeying the voice of the Lord as in the days when this nation was started. We say we love the United States of America, but we are doing everything we can to destroy this nation that we say we love. Look around and see, this nation is not great like it once was. We are not proud of this nation like we used to be. Why we don't even say the pledge to the American flag anymore. We haven't

saluted the flag during games or any where else I know of, for a long time. How can we say we love a country that we wont even salute or say a pledge to.

Behold we are trusting in the lying words that come from our leaders, knowing that they are lies, but still believing it as being the truth. This is coming from the President all the way down to the Governors of our beloved states. The people hear and would rather believe in a lie, then hold to the truth of our Lord, Christ Jesus. The only thing we are doing is provoking the Lord to bring upon us his wrath, and with that a lot of confusion of who or what we really are, or want to be. Come back to the Lord as your God, and see if he will not straighten out this country that we say we love so much.

As a nation we steal, murder, commit adultery, swear falsely, worship snakes and other animals. And yet stand it the pulpit and proclaim that the God of our fathers is not helping us at all. Have we forgotten what is in the Constitution, and how it was written with the Bible close by. But let the one that glorifies the Living God, glory in this: You understand and know Jesus the Christ, and that he exercises loving kindness, judgment and righteousness, not only in this country but in all countries around the world that we call home. For the Lord God of heaven and earth does not want to destroy this nation but that all nations should come to him and be saved.

AMERICA, DO WE REALLY LOVE HER?

Now therefore we know the law is good, but only if you use the law lawfully. We have those who desire to be teachers, and servants unto the law, but do not understand the law, or how to uphold the law. Knowing this, that the law is not made for the innocent person or people, but made for the disobedient person or people. The law has been written for the unholy people that commit murders, of our fathers, mothers and children, born or unborn. For man slayers, whore mongers,, and those who defile themselves with mankind. Also men stealer to sell as slaves or to make sure that they can make money of these people they kidnap or make them do things they wish not. For liars and perjured persons, and even those that are making the law is also committing these same crimes and many others.

So if we have nothing to hide, then we should not be afraid of the law. Therefore let us pray for our leaders and those in authority, that we all may lead a quiet and peaceful life. Let us be honest with each other, and let the person worship their God or gods without interfering with the worshiper of another religion or denomination. We say we love this nation, how about showing it by saying the pledge and standing up for the flag and what it represents.

STUPID MISTAKES

Everybody makes mistakes, we call these stupid mistakes.
We make these mistakes because we don't have knowledge.
Doctors, Lawyers, Bankers, and others have studied to know.
Unfortunately most of us think we know
more than professionals.
And when we try to out smart the professional we get hurt.
This is why we make mistakes, that we call stupid mistakes.
I have learned that a stupid mistake is actually just being stupid.
When we do not learn the lesson of making that stupid mistake.

WILLIAM T. SMITH

When we learn from our mistakes, then
that mistake is very valid.
But when we do not learn, then be
assured you will make another.
So do not put yourself down because of that stupid mistake.
Learn from it, and live a better life for the understanding of it.

William T. Smith

This is the one thing that our leaders I do believe forgot. This nation was built on a promise to be a free nation. But what happened over the past 75 to 80 years? This nation is not a dependent nation on our own resources, but we shut down our resources to buy the same from another country. This is not just a mistake, this was deliberate, so that the government could control us like it does in the third world nations. Wake-up citizens of this United States of America, look around and see what is going on. Then get the wisdom of what you see and start doing something about it that is wroth while.

This used to be a God fearing nation, we need to realize that something is wrong that the government can not fix. Controlling the people by religion, weapons, and over taxing them is not working. We elect these people to work for us to make this a better nation. All I see is trouble in this land, because it seems that our leaders wants to get rich over protecting our constitutional rights in this country we say we love.

Let us quit blaming everyone else for our troubles, and get back to the basics of our Constitution and the Bible. The Bible was the basics of our Constitution that worked for 200 years, why are we wanting to change the laws and bylaws in this document for something we have seen in other nations that did not work. We keep this up and the United States of America will not exist any more, it will be controlled by another country. When that happens we will not have these privileges that we love so dear.

AMERICA, DO WE REALLY LOVE HER?

Check your history books and see if what we are doing now ever worked! In every case in every country that went this way all failed. Why can't you see we are headed in the same direction? Please turn back to the Lord and start worshiping our beloved Savior. Yes! Jesus can and will do what our government has failed to do. Jesus will straighten out this whole mess if we will only come back into His grace. We have become a stiff-necked people and don't even realize what it is that we are doing. We are doing things that we know we should not, in every state and in every town. We are professing ourselves to be wise, in order to show that we are a bunch of fools.

Check out our Constitution and let us realize that we need these rights in order to be a great nation. Your freedom as well as mine may very well be in jeopardy if we don't wake-up. The church is a great place to start realizing this, the Bible will let you know if we are on the right tract.

In the words of our 22nd President Grover Cleveland "The teaching of Christ results in the purest Patriotism." Let's face it, without Christ as our leader in all things; we will fail at all things. If you don't believe this, your not looking at our country or our world; you can see it everywhere.

CHAPTER FIVE

I wrote some things about our country in three different books that are out or about to come out. These books are "Thoughts of William T. Smith" "I thank you Lord! I will say it in Poems, Psalms, Proverbs, Parables and plays" "Can you see God in Nature, Government, Home". I know I love this country, and the Lord for keeping it free for this long. In these thoughts I do not wish to put anybody down, even though sometimes it may seem that I am. Enjoy.

A THOUGHT FOR LEADERS

In Proverbs 14, there is a statement, all of us should borrow.
A large population is a King or President's prime glory.
If you take the way of the world, that deems to be right.
It very well may lead you into a very deathly fright.
If you seek wisdom, then you will have a heart of discerning.
Seek the advice of a wise counsel, let the wisdom be known.
The lips of the wise will spread knowledge with your prayers.
This will keep you safe and sound from worldly snares.
Things go wrong because they lack wisdom of a good counsel.
Seek wise counsel and advisers, listen to them, you will not fail.
When you have knowledge and
understanding, you are very wise.

AMERICA, DO WE REALLY LOVE HER?

You will have joy with all others who
seek healing and saving lives.

William T. Smith

I wrote because it seems to me that with all these abortions going on, that the glory of our President or Governor is not very wise in this. The population is going down and putting the burden of financing our country or state in jeopardy. The same with wise counsel that we do not have much of in our government. For the same thing is going on with illegal aliens, The citizen has to foot the bill for them to live here. This nation was built on aliens coming and making them a citizen of this country, they are called legal citizens not illegal aliens that do not wish to be an American but have all the privileges of a citizen. When you have knowledge with the wisdom of understanding, then you will want to save lives and not destroy lives, that makes a nation great and glorious.

AMERICA

When we sing America --- God will bless.
Why are we doing things that put us in a test.
How are we blessing our, Creator God.
When we worship idols on his sod.
God is all love and that is what we should make.
But we bless God of Heaven with intense hate.
God is all life and that is what we should murmur.
But we bless our God of life with murder.
God is all righteousness in that we should boost.
But we bless the God of Creation with our lust.
God is caring and in Jesus we have the seed.
But we bless the savior God with our greed.

WILLIAM T. SMITH

If we wish America to be great.
We need to confess our sin for her sake.
And when we praise Jesus Christ.
America will be great in his eyes.
If we want God's blessing, this is what to do.
Start praising Jesus for everything that is good.
Start glorifying Jesus as we should.
Start giving of ourselves like we could.
Ask Jesus to forgive us our sinful ways.
And always stand for Jesus all of our days.

William T. Smith

America, do we love her enough to say yes to the one who made her great and free. Jesus is the one we owe our freedom to, we should at least listen to what our religious leaders are saying about this freedom we have in our country and in our Lord Jesus Christ.

LET THE PRESIDENT DO HIS JOB

I know that President Trump is not a perfect President.
There are things in his pass that he probably like to forget.
Looking back one can see, this is true with all Presidents.
The Tabloids always want the worse and forget the best.
Why do the Tabloids like to print lies, more than the truth?
When they are not telling the truth, our trust in them we lose.
President Trump is doing what he can to make this nation great.
He cannot do his job as long as the press is always in the way.
He is trying to protect this country, that I believe he does love.
The press is mad because: he was asking for help from above.

AMERICA, DO WE REALLY LOVE HER?

Our President should want this nation to be great and powerful. So let the President do his job, for our country and your sake.

William T. Smith

I wrote this at a time when President Trump was being hounded by the press. It seemed that every time he started to do something, the press was making it look like he didn't know what he was doing. The experience that he had with dealing with foreign nations and companies I believe qualified him for that.

No matter who the President is, we should give him a little leeway to see what he can handle. If in fact he cannot handle the job, then it is up to us to remove that President from office. That is what elections are for.

PRAY FOR OUR PRESIDENT

Just as it was with the children of Jacob- Israel.
The U. S. A. citizens just want to have peace.
But it seems if the President stands for the nation.
The congress of this country will say "Impeach him".
But: if he talks to other countries and be a wimpy.
Congress will applaud the President for being weak.
But: if he stands tall and hold to his convictions.
Congress will call him a bully and cry impeach impeach.
We have been with a weak President, full of talk, no action.
He does not stand up for the country, and keeps us in debt.
Don't you think it is time for a concerned President.
Pray for our President, like him or not, we did elect him.
God says in His Word that He puts into power and takes out.
There is a reason Trump was taken out and Biden was put in.

WILLIAM T. SMITH

Pray for the President we have, that he
will make the right choice.
For with out prayer this will fall like Israel fell.

William T. Smith

Our President needs to have our prayers, in order to have grace upon this nation that we love so much. If we like our President or not, for the sake of our country we still must send up prayers, so that our country will survive this mess we are in.

PRESIDENT OBAMA

President Obama did not do much to impress me.
First, he said he was a Christian, then turned against Him.
It seems to me, that this is a type of the Antichrist.
And this country will definitely pay a high price.
When you look back on his terms as our President.
It seems to me, he was more for chaos and terrorism.
When you look back on what he did and wanted to do.
The freedom that we fought and cherish are taken from you.
I don't want you to think I hate President Obama, for I don't---
I am only pointing out that this country, he really didn't want.
If he cared about the people who voted him into the office.
He would have stopped the unnecessary
spending from congress.
Most of the laws and bills that the congress are passing.
Went against the Constitution of America and will not last.
As you probably know in the pass 24
years, this nation has went down.
More people have government programs; this is not very sound.
Now that President Trump is the new Commander in Chief.

AMERICA, DO WE REALLY LOVE HER?

War will be on the brink, with all this
mess President Obama left.
I believe President Trump is a man of his word, and of action.
And keeping this country strong and
safe, I believe is his passion.

William T. Smith

No! I do not care for President Obama administration, but I do not hate him, nor do I hate President Biden. I wish to see them in glory with me, but that decision is up to each of them. If they admit that Jesus is Lord God, and believe he rose from the grave, and is alive. Then all that is left is to ask Jesus to forgive them for the sins they committed, and forgive other that has done you wrong. That is all there is to it, do this with an honest heart and glory in heaven is yours.

PRESIDENT TRUMP

I heard a woman declare on the plane.
Good grief President Trump must be insane.
Trying to run this nation without any help of sort.
Without the help of congress or the Supreme Court.
Really he should not even be in the office of President.
Why! He doesn't even have any public consent.
But! If however you should come and ask me.
President Trump does have the right attitude and key.
The people has voted and with that vote have spoken.
And President he was elected and now that now is he.
Instead of expressing grief or resentment or complaining.
Why not start something new; we should start praying.
We all know President Trump is not infallible nor a king.
So start praying, and forget about all the complaining.

WILLIAM T. SMITH

No matter who our president is, he does need our support.
So that together we can make this nation great, of course.

William T. Smith

    I have found it is a lot easier to complain about a situation or about a person; than it is to pray and support the person we put in power to rule this nation. Complaining is easy, you don't like the person, or situation, or the person is of a different political party. Always remember this; the one that gets hurt the most, is the one that does the most complaining. The person that helps correct the situation or helps the person in power by simply praying for them becomes the hero in all of this, even though no one may know his or her name.

PRESIDENT TRUMP IN 2020

President Trump has been criticized a lot this term.
By the Legislators that has done worse, we have learned.
But: when we look back at the different Presidents.
The one we criticized the most. Is the one God has sent.
President Kennedy wanted our strength to be known.
He was assassinated for all the good will he showed.
He is now deemed as being a great President in history.
The country back then, did not know the whole story.
President Lincoln wanted peace and unity in our country.
War broke out and he was assassinated because of that.
His picture is on our pennies and five dollar bills.
He is recognized for what he stood for, by not quiting.
President Trump I do hope, will win a second term.
This country will be praised and glorified very soon.
Because he has grit in his bones and Jesus in his hand.
The congress wants to impeach him, I don't think it will stand.

AMERICA, DO WE REALLY LOVE HER?

If that does not work, his character will be assassinated.

William T. Smith

I was trying to point out that the presidents that we did not like at the time they were elected, is the same presidents that goes down in history as being great. That is because their ethics were in order with what written in the constitution, and second they had faith in the Lord to lead them in making the right decisions for the country they loved so much.

THE IMPEACHMENT

We are going through the impeachment of President Trump.
This impeachment has the country perplexed and stumped.
President Trump is elected; the Democratic
Party is mad, they lost.
Now everything they are doing, the citizens are paying the cost.
They have been at this for three long years, and found no cause.
It seems they keep bringing in false witnesses, that is tossed.
I have seen that no matter what the
President does for this country.
The congress will vote it down, the citizens pay the penalty.
When the President tries to make good on his promise to us.
The branches of government starts lying and put him to a test.
America can be great again, but we must all work together.
As long as we keep fighting within, this nation will be split.
Our country the USA and President needs our faithful prayers.
Not government control, but sacrifice and lots of tears.

William T. Smith

WILLIAM T. SMITH

Ever sense the 2nd world war, this country has been going downhill. That is when we started to kill our babies, the family unit was split and homosexual people was given the right to marry. All of this is the work of our enemy know as Satan or Devil. We are playing right into Satan's plan to bring down this country, simply because it was set -up on the principals laid out in the Bible. Satan always wants to do the opposite of God, that means any thing God has a hand in; Satan wants to destroy that thing. This is recorded in the Bible several times, but Satan always will fall short.

PRESIDENT NEEDS OUR PRAYERS

Our President has to make a lot of tough decisions.
Even though the Senate wants to impeach him.
I do believe he is doing what is best for America.
While making America great, he is keeping her safe.
The President does have a very hard and stressful job.
Sometimes he has to be like a card shark; hold the ace.
When it is safe, the people will know what is going on.
The President has to with-hold information for a while.
So we need to pray for our President, in all matters.
If we do this, you may find that his job can be bent.
While he is in power, his job is to protect the citizens.
In doing so, he has to make difficult choices for us.
He has a hard job to do without all the added stress.
Please pray for country and President that God will bless.

William T. Smith

AMERICA, DO WE REALLY LOVE HER?

     I wrote this with President Trump in mind, but it also goes with our present President also. No matter who our President is, he needs us to pray for him. It makes no difference if he is a good president, a bad president, or a puppet president; God is still in control and the Word tells us to pray for our leaders in all matters of government. If we are complaining about the President, that means we are not praying for him. If we don't pray for our president, then our enemies will be able to take over our country easier. Lets make it a practice to pray for the President every day, for he does need our prayers to run this nation.

TROUBLE IN THE USA

I believe that President Trump does not like ill-gotten gain.
For this reason, I do believe he will have a second reign.
I believe he also is faithful to the country, he will be blessed.
As for citizens of this country; violence need to be a rest.
The greedy people of this nation is stirring up this conflict.
They are causing a lot of problems and chaos and confusion.
The wicked politicians are taking bribes and there is no peace.
Do not be a mocker that stirs-up trouble, let the chaos cease.
It seems that the wicked is thriving, and, so is their evil sin.
The children of God that prays, will bring them to their knees.
The wicked are haughty and think they are pure in their eyes.
What they are saying and doing to mankind, is not very wise.
President Trump did not get the second term in the oval office.
But the Lord still has a plan, and God's plan will be carried out.

William T. Smith

WILLIAM T. SMITH

Sometimes I think we forget who is really in charge of things here on earth. We act like we are in charge of things, and leave the Lord God out of the situation. God created the earth and everything in it. But the Lord is the true God, he is the living God, and an everlasting king: at his wrath the earth shall tremble, and the nations shall not be able to abide his indignation. Thus you shall say unto them; The gods that have not made the heavens and earth, even they shall perish from the earth, and from under these heavens. He has made the earth by his power, he has established the world by his wisdom, and has stretched out the heavens by his discretion. Jeremiah 10: 10-12. All things will work out for the glory of God Almighty.

ARE YOU AMERICAN

There is one statement that I always hear.
I cringe when that statement comes to my ear.
The main statement is this: "I am an Afro-American".
The fact is: you were born in this nation, USA.
"I am a Russian-Japanese-Indian-Irish-American.
And yet you also was born in this nation, USA.
I can go with every ethic group in this country.
Why are you not wanting to accept, your American?
Are you being contrary because of your parents, or;
Do you think you would be better somewhere else?
It's your choice: choose America or your ancestors.
There are two ways to be a citizen of the USA.
The first is to be born here, that is natural citizenship.
The second is earned or declared for citizenship.
If you wish to be an American, then act like a citizen.
If you do not like it here, fine go back to your ancestors.
A United States citizen has rules and laws to live by.
Obey our laws, not the laws where your folks were born.

AMERICA, DO WE REALLY LOVE HER?

No matter if you are Black-White-Red-Yellow or Brown.
American is an American; be proud, follow our Constitution.

William T. Smith

Yes! If you love America, then show it by the way you respect America. Stand-up for our flag, and be proud to sing our National Anthem. This is our country, if you love it show it, if not get out to the country and to the one you do love. America may not be perfect, but: show me a country that is, if you can find one. Love this country and respect the laws and Constitution, that was set-up for liberty for all.

OUR RIGHTS

Lately I've seen on the news.
Our rights we are going to lose.
Look at what has happened in the past 20 Years.
We have already lost our rights, due to our fears.
We do not have the right of a doctor to choose.
For the government will choose and we will lose.
The rights we have as a normal citizen.
Is being taken away with criticism.
Our rights to carry a gun for protection.
Is being voted on by crooked politicians.
We murder our unborn children.
So our country cannot be protected from within.
We now have same sex marriage to support.
Our army doesn't have the strength in sort.
We are losing our rights, not because of President.
It is because we act like babies and need to be spanked.
If you need somebody to blame.

WILLIAM T. SMITH

Just look at yourself- you are lame.
A nation is as strong or weak by order.
By all the citizens within its border.

William T. Smith

We must stand-up and fight for our rights, that is given to us by our Constitution. It has been that way sense our nation became free. We fought for our freedom, are we willing to keep on fighting for our freedoms. We should not take our freedoms lightly, get a copy of the Constitution, learn it, and then fight to keep it. If we don't, then our freedoms will be lost forever and another country will take over this country. Where will we be then, while under the laws of a country that does not care about freedom or their citizens. Be careful and do not lose what we have fought so hard to keep.

FREEDOM

If I do what the Lord Jesus ask: then I am volunteering.
If I do what the Lord Jesus says I must do: It is a command.
I have the right of God, and country to do anything I please.
But: when I do this thing, is it being beneficial just to me?
I do have the right to do whatever I please in this earth.
But: doing whatever I please, may not be very constructive.
If I hurt someone, just because I am doing what I please.
Then what have I done to the rights of the other person.
When I say: I want to do the things pertaining to God?
Am I forcing you to do the same thing: No, I will not.
What I do, is because Of the freedom I have been given.
But: when my freedom keeps you from your freedom;
Then should I be free to do everything, just for me, and mine.

AMERICA, DO WE REALLY LOVE HER?

Or should I be considerate of your freedom also, and be meek.
I will not force you to believe in the Lord Jesus the way I do.
But: I will let you know about Him, so you can choose yourself.
Remember: I will not force my religion on you in any way.
I do not want you to force your religion on me either in any way.

William T. Smith

Freedom is a big word with a big definition: The quality or state of being free: as the absence of necessity, coercion, or constraint in choice or action. Liberation from slavery or restraint or from the power of another. Having Independence. The quality or state of being exempt or released usually from something onerous. The quality of being frank, open or out spoken. Having boldness of conception or execution. Unrestricted use. Privilege, Franchise, Freedom, Liberty, License. The power or condition of acting without compulsion. Yes freedom is a big word with a big meaning. Be careful how you use this word, it can help you or it can harm you; help you by keeping you free; or harm you by putting you behind bars. The choice is always up to you on how to use this freedom. But now being made free from sin, and become servants to God, you have your fruit unto holiness, and the end everlasting life. What shall we say then? Shall we continue in sin, that grace may abound? God forbid. How shall we, that are dead to sin, live any longer therein? Romans 6:22 & 6:1&2. Likewise we have our freedom by the Constitution, shall we then do whatever we please: God forbid that we should cause pain to someone else because of our misuse of our freedom in the Constitution or in the Lord God.

WILLIAM T. SMITH

PEOPLE OF USA

People of the USA come, let us walk in the light.
Let's ask for forgiveness and start doing what is right.
We have gone far away from our forefather's leading.
Turn back to Jesus, the light: This Faith Poet is pleading.
Our land is being filled with many strange religions.
People who say they know God; and turning a death ear.
Our land is filled with Silver, Gold and other treasure.
We are giving it to other countries at their pleasure.
When are we going to wake-up and take back our land?
From coast to coast, let her be strong and firmly stand.
This was once a great nation, one to be proud to live in.
What I see now is drugs, murder, chaos and terrorism.
What happened to this country in the past 75 years?
We turned away from Jesus, and we are reaping tears.
Jesus is in the business of forgiving, all we need to do is ask.
Jesus will turn this nation around like He did in the past.
When we ask for forgiveness; it must be with an honest heart.
Jesus knows if you are sincere or not, be honest from the start.

William T. Smith

This nation started out honoring the Lord, where our forefathers put their trust in the God that they choose to worship. We have been putting Jesus first in all things, and even though we did have problems and disagreed with different things. And when you check out the history of this nation of (USA) United States of America, you can see very well that God was with us through it all: That is until after the second World War. That is when we started to think we were better and smarter than our Creator God. I am the Lord your God; fear not: for I am with you; I have loved you from the beginning.

AMERICA, DO WE REALLY LOVE HER?

For everyone that is called by my name: I have created that person for my glory, I have formed him; yes, I have made him. But you have departed out of the way; you have caused many to stumble, for you have not kept my ways, and dealing treacherously with every man and not remembering that one God created all of us. For by God was all things created, that is in heaven, and that is in earth, visible or invisible, whether it be thrones, or dominions, or principalities, or powers: all things were created by him, and for him. And in Christ Jesus is all treasures of wisdom and knowledge hidden, and the mystery of God, and the Father, and of Christ are knitted together in love, unto the riches of full assurance of understanding, to the acknowledgement of God through Christ Jesus.

NATION OF THE FREE

There is a good reason we are called: Land of the Free.
But: lately I have been asking: How long will this be?
The politicians are trying to take these rights away.
The people of this country wants terrorism, they say.
Half of the first Amendment is almost gone it seems.
As the politicians are saying: We do not want religion.
The second Amendment is going way out of our sight.
Wanting to take our guns, so the unlawful we cannot fight.
The fourth Amendment will soon be gone, having no affect.
The government can come in and seize without a warrant.
Article one section nine is being violated by Congress.
They take money from Social Security without permission.
Also--- Congress is passing bills not good for the citizens.
Is Congress doing what is right for this nation to stay free?
Get your copy of the Constitution of the United States.
See for yourself, Are they for you? Or for themselves?
Go to the polls and vote for a candidate of your choice.
Lets take back America through the elections of this nation.

WILLIAM T. SMITH

It works a whole lot better than riots with chaos and destruction. Lets go back to what has been working for a long time: election.

William T. Smith

The reason that our forefathers stood and fought against England; is the same reason that America is having all these problems. England took away the rights of the colonist and started to have them do things that was against their faith and their way of life. Look around at the country now, Is that what is going on here in this country? Things that is in the Constitution are being changed to fit the life style of the ones we have elected. And the citizen that they have promised to serve and protect, are having there rights taking away from them, and even the security of the elderly is being stolen from them. What started out not being controlled by the government; is now part of the government that we call Congress. Yes: the government is taking more control and the citizens are getting less representation;

Not at all what our forefathers wanted for this new country that they fought and died for. Get a copy of the Constitution and study it so that you wont fall for the illegal laws that Congress is wanting to pass, that will take away the rights that we have in this nation.

CHAPTER SIX

Here are a few more thoughts that I have written; Hope you will like them and understand why we need these different rights to exist.

GUN CONTROL

Take away guns from private citizens, and you will get this;
Gunmen in the streets, knowing the
victim cannot protect himself.
You will find killers and thieves in all kinds of public places.
The sour note of not being able to fight back, leaves a sour taste.
Only in America will crooks run wild,
and the innocent punished.
How can we defend ourself, if the
government wants our weapons.
The Constitution declares that we have the right to bare arms.
When we cannot, then a lot of innocent people will get harmed.
We have the right to protect ourself from those who are lawless.
Members of the government does not
wish that we protect ourselves.
Instead of getting the weapons away from known crooks hands.
They want the guns from us law-abiding citizens of this land.
So my question is this: Does the government
want to help the people?

WILLIAM T. SMITH

Or: Does the government want another
country take over this nation?
For without the private citizen having
weapons to protect themselves;
How are we going to stop another nation
from taking over, Do you know?

William T. Smith

Even Jesus told his disciples to sell their coat and buy a sword to help protect themselves in time of trouble. Being Jesus our Lord and Savor knew we needed weapons, why is it that the government wants to take our weapons. Trouble is coming, as you see in every town in every State of this great nation. But if we cannot protect ourself in times of trouble; what will come of this great nation of ours?

To our elected officials in the government; please use some common sense in running this nation the way our forefathers and our Lord God wants it ran.

TROUBLE IN THE USA

The citizens are being oppressed in this country.
It started slow, but now it is becoming outlandish.
Back in the 50's the Bible was taken out of schools.
To be replaced with what? "The Big Bang Theory".
The Ten Commandments was removed from court yards.
To have morals these days is very, very hard to find.
We have the people crying that do not want religion.
Drug abuse, abortions and sex traffic are ever so strong.
A run on the borders of this country is very evident.

AMERICA, DO WE REALLY LOVE HER?

This nation is being split, and cannot stand for very long.
The question now is: How do we get out of this total mess?
We must repent; tear down our strong holds and pagan alters.
Turn back to God, like our money says: "In God We Trust".
Do this and we may have peace again within our nation.
A country without God, is a country bound for failure.
A country with God, will end up great and strong.

William T. Smith

All through history you will find that the nations that reverenced God, by doing what they knew was right to do for their citizens, always fared well and usually was at peace with other nations. It was the nations that refused to live by the laws that was set before them, these are the ones that tries to control the world by making war with their neighbors. They are never satisfied with being friendly, but having control of other nations, that only causes strife and chaos with their neighboring nations, as well as the nations around the world. Look around at this nation and you will find those same traits with our leaders; first they want the nation to leave God; Second they want to control the citizens that they represent, by taking away the rights their fathers and grandfathers fought and possibly died for. Third they will want to control the nations around them. One way to do this is by letting illegals into the nation; I am not opposed to immigrants coming into this nation of ours; as long as they do it legally and obey the laws and the Constitution, to become a citizen of this great nation.

WILLIAM T. SMITH

SANCTUARY CITIES

I have heard a lot about sanctuary cities: What are they?
The dictionary has two definitions for these sanctuaries.
The first one: A place or refuge for protection in a city.
The second: The immunity from law, attached to sanctuary.
The Bible in Numbers 35 says it in a little different format.
It is a place a person can go for protection until the trail.
If the person is found guilty of the crime, he is punished.
If he is innocent, he can stay there and be protected by law.
The way the cities and states has it surmised now a days is:
We are going to protect him from punishment, no matter what.
Even if that person does crimes against that state or country.
A sanctuary city should not protect criminals, being a safety net.
When a state refuses to punish the guilty by harboring them.
Then that city or state is guilty of crimes against America.
Just because the person is alien, they are not above the law.
The law is to protect the innocent, and prosecute the guilty.

William T. Smith

I do believe that we have our laws all backwards at times; the one we should be protecting is the one that we want to punish; and the one that should be punished is the one we are protecting. Sanctuary cities are good, if they are used in the proper way. We do have the witness protection agency, that protects a guilty person in order to punish the ringleaders of the guilty. As long as that guilty person stays out of trouble, I do believe it is okay to protect that person from their partners, in order to protect our innocent citizens.

AMERICA, DO WE REALLY LOVE HER?

A NATION THAT IS LOST

Sometimes I get discouraged and think that all is lost.
Then I remember, I was put here for a reason a cause.
This life that I live, keeps me in turmoil, being tossed.
It was for me and you that Jesus was put on the cross.
What I am seeing is a forward generation, with no taste.
Children believing there is no God, not having any faith.
A nation that have representatives, but has no council.
Neither is there any wisdom or understanding in them.
What is missing? The "Rock of our salvation" Jesus our God.
The rock we trust in, is not the true Rock, but it is Satan.
Vengeance and recompense belongs to the Lord Jesus.
We wonder; where is this God of gods that we trusted in?
Oh: that we should let Jesus be our shelter, yes! Our refuge.
People of USA, be happy and be saved by the "God of Truth".
Let us rest in the everlasting arms of our God (Christ Jesus).
Let the Shield and the Sword of the Almighty go before us.

William T. Smith

Yes! This nation at one time was worshiping Christ Jesus the risen Lord. Our forefathers wrote about Lord Jesus in the Constitution and other places. Yes! When they gave a speech they always included something about our Savior. They had morals and also council, with that they had the wisdom and understanding to start a new nation. One that was free to worship the god of their choice. They were not perfect nor did they have all the answers; but they did seek wise council and they also searched the Word; which is the Holy Bible. If our leaders of today did this same thing, what a difference it would make. But look and read the articles that are being passed in Congress in the last several years. Does any of them honor or glorify the Lord Jesus, No! These articles and laws promote things that our forefathers were against. Wake-up USA and see what is going on in our government- in our churches- and yes even in our homes.

THE UNITED STATES COIN

Our coin says: In God We Trust.
So the world, we should not lust.
If Jesus Christ is really our Savior.
Then in Jesus- should be our labor.
The only things that will last.
Is what we do for our Lord, Christ.
The things here on earth we covet.
Is like putting water in a rusty bucket.
When we illegally get wealthy lot.
You usually find it is really for naught.
When we work for the Lord of Host.
In Christ Jesus we will be able to boast.
Let us continually do what is right.
And for Jesus, we can truly fight.
For only when we serve Him.
Will we be able to really win.

William T. Smith

Our government put on our money; "In God We Trust" and I believe they did that because: they really wanted to trust in God more than in themselves. If I were to guess; I would have to say that none to nearly none of our elected officials even owns a Bible, let alone setting down to read what is in this book of God. Yes:

AMERICA, DO WE REALLY LOVE HER?

We used to believe in the Almighty God; and would reverence God in our life, with our money, and in our homes and businesses. Something we rarely see these days, is honesty, love for one another or any type of morals. We should fight for our nation, and we should also give that fight back to the Lord. For only through our Lord Jesus will we win this moral fight that we have with our government. We need to pray for our leaders and ask Jesus to reveal to our leaders the correct way to run this nation; God's way.

COVID-19

We are in hard times now, and there are blames and pity.
We are afraid of what might happen, if we go into the city.
But the trouble came, and we are becoming very discouraged.
We have faltering knees, that cannot keep us, when we stumble.
We do pity and blame ourselves and
forget about being confident.
As we are blaming everyone around us,
knowing they are innocent.
We put on masks and stay six feet apart,
hoping to avoid all others.
We even stay away from family, not
seeing our sisters and brothers.
We stay at home in the hope this virus
"COVID-19" will go away.
We forget that God is in charge, so we
complain and cry, no praying.
As we listen to the news with all the
politicians promising complaints.
Trying to fix a disease with politics,
there's no faith or cures that can.

William T. Smith

WILLIAM T. SMITH

When this pandemic hit the only thing we thought about was: Where did this virus come from? How are we going to punish those who started this? Along with these two questions was also the statement that this is just a hoax; or this is another way the government wants to control the citizens of this country. I for one still think there was more going on then just these two scenario's, I may personally never know what it really was, but my Lord Jesus does know. You see Jesus was in charge of the outcome of this virus, even before it happened. Jesus also allowed it to happen, because God had a bigger plan in store for all of this. It was a hard year, and going through this pandemic caused us to actually learn from it; but like all the other lessons that we had to learn down through history, we will forget and do the same old things over again.

THE PETITION

I got a letter that said please do not ignore.
The politicians is taking our money for sure.
Into their pockets it will stay and be stored.
So they can have fancy homes and cars a galore.
I should not have to give money or sign a petition.
If our officials were being honest politicians.
If they would do the job that they were hired.
Then the retired folks life would be better by far.
You know they are taking our money to buy steak.
While we are trying to live on nothing but fish bait.
While they are living in a big house on a hill.
Our children say live with me, don't want you to steal.
So why should an outsider that I should pay.
When it seems the politicians has the final say.
If they cannot do their job, let it be their loss.
Come election time, replace them- we are the boss.

William T. Smith

AMERICA, DO WE REALLY LOVE HER?

The politicians wants the title of being our representative, but to remember why they were elected they seem to have forgotten. When one of our elected officials start doing this, why do we keep electing them into office. They are suppose to be working for the citizens that elected them into that office. So do not reelect someone that you know will not work for you, but for themselves. We elected that person we can vote someone else into office, hoping that this person will work for us, and not get polluted with all the money that is floating around Washington DC. We have the right to vote someone in; we also have the right to vote someone out. Let us start showing the politicians who there boss is, write to them and let them know how you feel about the issues at hand.

OUR COUNTRY

Here is a statement from our 35th President of USA.
President Kennedy; I believe strongly in what he said.
Here it is, "Ask not what your country can do for you;
But: what can you do for your country". A true statement.
Is this what we are asking ourselves from this President.
How can we help the one God put in power; one God sent?
What we are asking now is: What can I get from this country?
Even illegals want a handout, not doing things for themselves.
Is the freedom to be an American, a thing of the past?
If we keep taking from the country, how long will it last?
Wake-up people of this country--- we that are blessed.
The way we are going; this country will soon be cursed.
Lets start working for our country, lets keep our freedom.
Instead of law suits to bring down; lets uplift the President.

William T. Smith

WILLIAM T. SMITH

 I have seen a lot of corruption in the government these past few elections. The elect to be will say almost anything, just to get elected. After that they forget the citizen and start doing project that has nothing to do with running this country of ours. Then instead of running the country, we have lawsuits and illegals coming in for handouts. The citizens of this country should be taken care of first, not that we can not help the illegals, but don't take away from our citizens what belongs to them.

IS THIS OUR LAND?

Here in the USA we have a saying where we boast.
Disaster will not overtake us, nor will it ever meet us.
I believe the Lord has sworn by Himself the pride of Jacob.
If our country keeps sinning, we will drink the wrath cup.
The pride in our heart, has deceived us to think this way.
Who can bring this nation down, who can take our bliss?
Even though we make homes in the high, with the clouds.
And have fields and orchards a plenty, of this we are proud!
The countries that set at our table is really taking over.
   We think we are smart and don't know
     to look over our shoulder.
It wont be long, and America will not belong to citizens like us.
We will work and pay tribute to another country, without a fuss.

William T. Smith

 Yes: this country is being taking over by other countries, and it seems like we don't care. Look around and see how many big businesses have been bought out by foreign companies. If this keeps up Americans will be employed by other countries; how long will it take for those countries start telling us what we can do

AMERICA, DO WE REALLY LOVE HER?

or say. Somewhere along the way, we have been blinded by how the world thinks in 3rd world countries. We are in so deep now, that I cannot see a way out of this mess; printing more money is not the solution to this problem. That is helping other countries to be able to take our this country without firing a shot. The pride of Americans is going to be our downfall, We think we can do anything we please and not have to take the consequence of our action. This is wrongful thinking but; unfortunately the leaders of this country cannot see what is going on in the world today. Either that or they know and doing their best to make it happen. Either way we the citizens are going to be the big losers in this battle.

THIS COUNTRY

The corn is growing tall, with trees in the background.
Everything I am looking at, is very beautiful and sound.
The American flag is flying in the wind off the porch.
And nature is moving about doing their daily chores.
This is the life I live, I love this country that I live in today.
And our soldiers gave their lives, so I can live this way.
Do we really know and remember what they have done.
So we can live in a country with peace, and enjoy fun.
This country has been bought with a lot of pain and tears.
So that we can live in peace and not have death fears.
What has happened to this country, over the past few years.
All I see now is destruction, with riots and chaos very near.
Oh: How I long for us to know and remember our history.
How we used to praise the Lord in our churches without fear.

William T. Smith

WILLIAM T. SMITH

The constitution states that we have many different rights; The ones that is in power is wanting to take these rights away because of something that happened to them or their family. If these people would step back and look at the full picture, I believe if they did they would find out that some of the laws they made were against the constitution in the first place. One of these is taking the Bible out of our schools, and taking anything that had to do with Christian religion off of the courtyards because it might offend someone. Doing all of this did offend someone, many someones that may or may not spoke against the removal of these things.

A BLESSED NATION

We have came a long way in this blessed nation.
As every person knows of the blessed sensation.
We started with 13 states on the eastern shore.
Now we have 48 states all the way to the western shore.
With Alaska and Hawaii being the last two off shore.
This is a land of plenty, and people are wanting more.
With this some have figured they need to ripoff the poor.
The poor that is getting ripped off, is not blessed any more.
Other countries know that we are very well blessed.
Some wants to come here and live, others just envy us.
No matter where you live; you can also be very blessed.
Turn to Jesus as your God, you can also be a blessing.
All you need to do is accept Jesus Christ as your God.
We will be blessed, as long as we do things God's way.
When the time comes when we think we are not blessed.
Look back at the ungodly things we have done, then pray.

William T. Smith

AMERICA, DO WE REALLY LOVE HER?

In the past 250 years this country has came a long way. We have 50 states and 5 move if I am correct that would like to become states. As long as God is in this country I do believe we will prosper, We have been taking God out of this country, and look at what is happening- Abortions- Same sex marriages- Sex identity- and all kinds of evil things going on. Jesus said that whosoever followed him, he would in no way cast out. This country is not following Jesus and he will cast this nation out; It wont be long before you see this happen more than we see it now.

THIS LAND

As the sun comes up in the east, It will surly set in the west.
While we on earth, will keep living and trying to do our best.
We were created by God to take care of this planet we live on.
Our life span is short as it seems, we wont be here for long.
The farmer grows fields of vegetables, wheat, bean and corn.
Ranchers raise cattle, sheep, and other animals that are foreign.
Lumberjacks cut down trees for
production while planting more.
We are trying to take of this earth we live on, that is for sure.
The wars we fight has become very destructive, in all this land.
Afterwards we do try and rebuild, but;
nothing is really the same.
I do believe that we often forget who is
in charge, it is our Creator.
While we go about doing our own thing, trying to get a lot more.
The earth was created for man to live on, to take of, and to use.
Most of the time as it seems, we want
to fight each other and abuse.
Let us turn back to our Creator, God Almighty and live his way.
The earth is only being borrowed while
living here, we cannot stay.

WILLIAM T. SMITH

One day we will die and be buried in
this earth, as we turn into dust.
Look to Jesus who is the author and finisher
of our existence, it's a must.

William T. Smith

God created this world as well as the universe that surrounds this world. We have been looking into space and the main thing we have found is this: Our world that we call earth is the only livable world out in the space we know. That should tell us that what is in the Bible is true; and what is written on those pages will indeed happen. We are here for a short time and the only thing that will last is what we have done for Jesus. You don't believe that what I said is true or have any stretchability to it; look at the country of Israel, God blessed that nation where it was the greatest nation in the world. This nation was so great that they removed God from it; it wasn't long before the nation was so corrupt that God removed the nation from the earth. 2000 years later God blessed the people and now it is a nation again. So I will ask you if you would pray for this nation and please bring Jesus back as the one we are trusting in.

OUR NATION

In the mist of sticks and stones and all the rubble.
This country is most certainly in very deep trouble.
Yes: the politicians and our other elected officials.
They are the sticks and the stones of this nation, that talks.
We the citizens of this country, have become the rubble.
That our officials leave behind them, like corn stubble.
Question: How can this nation continue to stand;

AMERICA, DO WE REALLY LOVE HER?

When we are tossed around like the waves of ocean sand?
Question: How can this nation again be great and strong;
When migrates does not want this nation to them belong?
Question: With all of this; How can this nation be great?
Let us come together as a nation, for this nations sake.
Let the politicians complain, while not doing their job.
And in doing so, we become a split nation, a broken cog.
Being split we will never be great, nor ever be united.
We are being defeated by our own selfish greedy acts.
Yes: this nation can become strong, and can be great.
Let us come together as one nation; for our country's sake.
Let us get back to the beginning, when God was first.
Let Jesus be known far and wide to lift this sin curse.

William T. Smith

This great nation of ours is split in half, by the way the politicians cannot agree on anything. If someone disagree they want to either bring charges against that person; or they try to impeach that person. We are spending more time and money on lawsuits and impeachments then we are try to get tis nation moving again. The money wasted on these things could be used to maintain roads, or used to help those that are in need of help. Our citizens fought to keep this country free, and we will not even help our veterans to live well or have good medical treatment.

LIVING IN ILLINOIS

In central Illinois, where I was born and raised.
Fields grow green and the cattle in fields do graze.
Most towns are small villages, cities in comparison.
Where we look up in the sky, and see stars and sun.

WILLIAM T. SMITH

Where the folks around town, knows almost everyone.
What each family is, and what they are doing and done.
There is a lot of wide open spaces, living in the country.
We travel the country side,live stock and nature we see.
All in one, we are no different from big city dwellers.
We work, play and live to buy things from the sellers.
At the end of the day we go home, by bus, train or driving.
We all need a savior, mine is our Creator God (Lord Jesus).
What is the god you serve, is it things, job, or maybe family?
Ask Jesus into your life! For all of His creation is blessed.

William T. Smith

Yes I do like living in Illinois, where like most of central United States is basically has the same layout. There are fields all around, and cattle farms just about everywhere, in my humble opinion this still is the best state to live in. But like the city folk we have a lot of stress in our life as we work, play, and live out our life in the place we like best. The main thing here is that we all have an opportunity to serve the Creator God in the same way. For there is only one way to serve Creator God and that is to accept the Son Jesus as your Lord and Savior who will forgive your sin. You do this with an honest and open heart, for Jesus already knows if you mean what you are praying. I will ask if you would please pray for our leaders, not just on the Federal level but also on the State level.

THE FUTURE

We all wonder what our future world will be like!
When you read Revelation, the secret you can find.
You must read it as it is written, line by each line.

AMERICA, DO WE REALLY LOVE HER?

For the future is told, but: not for all to understand.

The financial will be one bank, as I perceive it to be.
Fiscal money will be no good, only an account you see.
The way Revelation reads, you will know what you have.
No matter where in the world you live or country your at.

The health system is one that will be difficult to understand.
No service will be given, if you cannot access the account.
Because the bank and the health department goes hand in hand.
No matter what your health looks like, no treatment is found.

As for the government there will be only one for all.
One man will be in charge, the government is his call.
The financial as well as the health system, is under his rule.
The account you have at the bank is for everything everywhere.

But: the religion will be with the school where you are sent.
One religion ruled by one, school, ruled by one government.
I know that this may sound like a bunch of humble jumble.
But: read the book of Revelation closely, you may see reality.

William T. Smith

I know this is a little different, but: I felt that we should know what is in store for all earth, for the times that are coming. I cannot tell you when this will happen, so I am letting you know what to look for, so you can get prepared for it. Personally I feel that the time is getting close for these events to happen, which means it could start at any time, but could hold off for a while so more people can become a child of the living God. But mark my words now; it will most certainly happen, for the Bible declares it to happen, and God does not lie.

WILLIAM T. SMITH

Jesus is standing at the door of your heart today.
Will you let Him in before it is too late?

How to become a Christian

JESUS OF NAZARETH

Jesus Christ was with God the Father before the world was created. He became human and lived among humanity as Jesus of Nazareth. He came to show us what God the Father is like. He lived a sinless life, showing us how to live; and He died upon a cross to pay for our sins. God raised Him from the dead.

Jesus is the source of eternal life. Jesus wants to be the doorway to new life for you. In the Bible He was called the "Lamb of God" (John 1:29). In the Old Testament, sacrifices were made for the sins of the people. Jesus became the sacrificial lamb offered for your sin.

Jesus said, "I am the way, the truth, and the life. No one comes to the Father except through Me" (John 14:6). He is waiting for you now.

* Admit to God that you area sinner. Repent.
* Repent, turning away from your sin.
* By faith receive Jesus Christ as God's Son.
* Accept Jesus' gift of forgiveness from sin.
* He took the penalty for your sin by dying on the cross.
* Confess your faith in Jesus Christ as Savior and Lord.

You may pray a prayer similar to this as you call on God to save you; But do it with an honest heart in faith believing Jesus is the Son of the living God:

AMERICA, DO WE REALLY LOVE HER?

"Dear God, I know that You love me. I confess my sin and need of salvation. I turn away from my sin and place my faith in Jesus as my Savior and Lord. In Jesus' name I pray, Amen".

After you have received Jesus Christ into your life, tell a pastor or another Christian about your decision. Show others your faith in Christ by asking for baptism by immersion in your local church as a public expression of your faith.

On a finial note; here is a thought about our flags. If you love your country then please fly your flag to let people know. If you love your God or gods then fly the Christian flag or the flag of your god if you have one.

COUNTRY AND CHRISTIAN FLAG

In all the churches we should have our country's flag showing.
Along beside it should also be the Christian flag also showing.
Our country's flag shows that we do actually love our country.
Our Christian flag that we love our
Lord and Savior; or your god.
This should mean that we will obey the laws of our country.
Also, we should obey the laws of God, as recorded in our Bible.
We may not agree with the laws of our country, but we will obey.
The Bible does not say we should agree with all laws; just obey.
The law of God is laid out very clear on
what we should do and say.
There are ten laws or commandments
that is in the Word of God.
They are in two parts: Love your God, and Love your neighbor.
On these two laws or commandments hang all the law of God.
The laws of our country are made to protect all of the citizens.
The laws of God are there to forgive the sins of all sinners.

WILLIAM T. SMITH

Who is a citizen of our country? The one
that belongs to our country.
So: who is a sinner? The one that belongs
to earth, by being born here.
That is if your are an earthling, then you
are a sinner born on earth.
A sinner is one that has worldly lust, that they must live out.
Jesus came to this world to redeem the sinful people of earth.
He did not come to condemn mankind,
but to save the mankind.
He does that by having you to believe on the Son Christ Jesus.
Believe that He is the Savior of mankind, and forgives your sin.
When you believe and ask Jesus to forgive you of your sins.
Then you become a citizen of God and
heaven, living on this earth.
When you do, you become an ambassador
for Jesus and Christianity.
You will live on earth, but your citizenship
is with God in his heaven.

William T. Smith

If you love this country, then you should be praying for this country. The best way to pray for this country is to give your heart and soul to God; and ask Jesus to forgive you of your sin. Then your prayer will have more effect on being answered; for you will then have a direct line to God's throne.

Jesus' last prayer
John 16:31 to 17:26 & 20:21-23

AMERICA, DO WE REALLY LOVE HER?

Jesus answered them, Do you now believe? Behold the hour comes, yes, is now come, that you shall be scattered, every man to his own house, and shall leave me alone: and yet I am not alone, because the Father is with me. These things I have spoken unto you, that in me you might have peace.

In the world you shall have tribulation: but be of good cheer; I have overcome the world.

These words spake Jesus, and lifted up his eyes to heaven, and said, Father, the hour is come; glorify your Son, that your Son also may glorify you: As you have given power over all flesh, that he should give eternal life to as many as you have given him. And this is life eternal, that they might know you the only true God, and Jesus Christ, whom you have sent. I have glorified you on earth: I have finished the work which you gave me to do.

And now, O Father, glorify you in me with your own self with the glory which I had with you before the world was. I have manifested your name unto the men which you gave me out of the world: yours they were, and you gave them to me; and they kept your word. Now they have known that all things whatsoever you have given me of you. For I have given unto them the words which you gave me; and they have received them, and have known surely that I came out from you, and they have believed that you did send me.

I pray for them: I pray not for the world, but for them which you have given me; for they are yours. And all mine are yours, and yours are mine; and I am glorified in them. And now I am no more in the world, but these are in the world, and I come to you. Holy Father, keep through your own name those whom you have given me, that they may be one, as we are one.

While I was with them in the world, I kept them in your name: those that you gave me I have kept, and none of them is lost, but the son of perdition (or the son of destruction); that the scripture might be fulfilled. And now come I to you; and these things I speak in the world, that they have ,my joy fulfilled in themselves. I have given them your word; and the world have hated them, because they are not of the world, even as I am not of the world.

I pray not that you should take them out of the world, but that you should keep them from the evil of this world. They are not of this world, even as I am not of this world. Sanctify them through your truth: your word is truth. As you have sent me into the world, even so have I also sent them into the world. And for their sakes I sanctify myself, that they also might be sanctified through the truth.

Neither pray I for these alone, but for them also which shall believe on me through their word;

That they all may be one; as you, Father, are in me, and I in you, that they also may be one in us; that the world may believe that you have sent me. And the glory which you gave me I have given them; that they may be one, even as we are one: I in them, and you in me, that they may be made perfect in one; and that the world may know that you have sent me, and have loved them,as you have loved me.

Father, I will that they also, whom you have given me, be with me where I am; that they may behold, my glory, which you have given me: for you loved me before the foundation of the world. O righteous Father, the world has not known you: but I have known you, and these have known that you have sent me. And I have declared unto them your name, and will declare it: that the love wherewith you have loved me may be in them, and I in them.

There is no Amen or anything to close this prayer; for this prayer was left open for Jesus to finish while he was on the cross. When Jesus said "it is finished": in John 19:30, that ended his earthly prayer for all generations. With that Jesus paid the price for our sin here on earth; all we have to do is ask

Jesus to forgive us for the disobedience to God the Father. Jesus did not finish there, He also breathed on us the Holy Spirit.

In the book of Ecclesiastes 4:8-12, this is what is written: There is one alone, and there is not a second; No, he has neither child or brother: yet is there no end of all his labor; neither is his

AMERICA, DO WE REALLY LOVE HER?

eye satisfied with riches; neither said he, For whom do I labor, and bereave (deprived) my soul of good? This is also vanity, Yes, it is sore travail (torture).

Two are better than one: because they have a good reward for their labor. For if they fall, the one will lift up his fellow: but woe to him that is alone when he falls; for he has not another to help him up.

Again, If two lie together, then they have heat: but how can one be warm alone? And if one prevail against him, two shall withstand him; and a threefold cord is not quickly broken.

This is what Jesus was saying in his prayer; the Father is in Jesus; Jesus is in the Christian; the Christian in the Father as well as in Jesus. That makes me part of a threefold cord, and this cord is not quickly broken.

Jesus did not stop there, no not by a long shot. When you look into John 20:21-23 Jesus tells us this: Then Jesus said unto them again, Peace be unto you: as my Father has sent me, even so I send you.

And when he had said this, he breathed on them, and said unto them, Receive you the Holy Spirit: Whose soever sins you remit (forgive what they did to you), they are remitted (not holding a grudge) unto them; and whose soever sins you retain (remember), they are retained (held accountable for).

Jesus is telling us to forgive your fellow person just as he has forgiven you; do not hold a grudge or do not hold that person accountable to you for their action. With this the cord he was talking about is not a threefold cord; but now it is a fourfold cord: the Father in Jesus, Jesus in the Christian, the Christian in the Holy Spirit, the Holy Spirit in the Father. The Father, Lord Jesus, Holy Spirit, and the Christian (Child of God). This is a fourfold cord that is impossible to break. Why? God has ordained it to be this way; if not we would be tossed from one side to another.

The way I look at Jesus' last prayer
William T. Smith

www.ingramcontent.com/pod-product-compliance
Lightning Source LLC
LaVergne TN
LVHW061039070526
838201LV00073B/5111